Television & Ethics

A Bibliography

Television & Ethics

A Bibliography

Thomas W. Cooper

with
Robert Sullivan
Christopher Weir
Peter Medaglia

G. K. Hall & Co.
Boston

Citations and/or abstracts are derived from:

Magazine Index[tm] and Trade & Industry Index[tm] © 1987 by Information Access Company, Belmont, California. Material reproduced by permission of the publisher.

ABI/INFORM, the business database. © UMI/Data Courier. The full text of the articles abstracted in ABI/INFORM is available from UMI/Data Courier at $9.50 U.S. per article in the U.S. and Canada. To place an order, call 800/626-2823 in the U.S. and 800/626-0307 in Canada.

American Psychological Association, publisher of *Psychological Abstracts* and the PsycInfo Database (© 1967-87 by the American Psychological Association). Reprinted with permission of the American Psychological Association. This material may not be reproduced without its prior permission.

Sociological Abstracts, San Diego, California. Material reproduced with permission of *Sociological Abstracts.* Abstracts have been edited. No material may be reprinted without its prior approval.

Copyright 1988 by Thomas W. Cooper and Emerson College.
Published by G.K. Hall & Co.
A Division of Macmillan, Inc.
All rights reserved.

Library of Congress Cataloging in Publication Data

Cooper, Thomas W. (Thomas William), 1950-
Television and ethics: bibliography / Thomas W. Cooper, compiler; Peter Medaglia, managing editor; Robert Sullivan, research editor; Christopher Weir, business editor.
p. cm.
Includes indexes.
ISBN 0-8161-8966-8
1. Television broadcasting--Moral and ethical aspects--Bibliography. 2. Ethics--Bibliography. I. Medaglia, Peter. II. Sullivan, Robert. III. Weir, Christopher. IV. Title.
Z7711.C66 1988
[PN1992.6]
174'.97914--dc19   88-7206

For Michael, Nancy, Nancie
Clifford, and Lisa

CONTENTS

THE EDITORS

Dr. Thomas W. Cooper received his B.A. magna cum laude from Harvard University in Visual and Social Studies in 1973. As an assistant to Marshall McLuhan, playwright, and author, he received his M.A. and Ph.D. at the University of Toronto in Theater and Communication. Founding director of the Association for Responsible Communication, Cooper has hosted several international teleconferences among media professionals worldwide, as sponsored by AT&T, the International Communication Association, Harvard, and other organizations. His faculty position in Mass Communication at Emerson College follows similar teaching assignments at the University of Maryland, Temple University, and Harvard. Cooper's numerous books and articles have been published by such wide-ranging publishers and publications as Longman, Inc., *Journalism Quarterly, The Journal of Communication, Film Quarterly, Journal of Mass Media Ethics, Nieman Reports, Film Criticism,* and *The Harvard Crimson.* He was recently a guest of Moscow State University as lecturer to the Department of Journalism and has been the recipient of many grants, awards, and special honors.

Robert Sullivan was educated at Bridgewater State College and Emerson College. He is the head of the Reference Department at the Emerson College Library and an adjunct instructor at Emerson College. He has lectured on communication topics at other colleges and universities and acted as a consultant on corporate communications and marketing for a variety of firms.

Christopher Weir, A.B. Duke University, M.A. Emerson College, was Vice President, Account Management, at BBDO International in New York for sixteen years prior to managing his own advertising agency in Western Connecticut. For the past five years, he has served in administrative roles at Emerson College, where he is also adjunct professor of advertising. Weir moderated and coproduced both Telev..sion and Ethics Conferences hosted by Emerson College and is copublisher and coeditor of the conference proceedings.

Peter Medaglia, received his M.A. degree in 1986 in Writing and Publishing from Emerson College where he managed computer operations for major searches used in producing this bibliography. He has since become a manager in the direct mail business.

Advisory Editors

Clifford G. Christians
Eugene Goodwin
J. Michael Kittross
Donald L. McBride
Robert Roberts
Christopher Sterling

Contributors

Clifford G. Christians
Eric Elbot
Deni Elliott
John P. Ferre
Eugene Goodwin
James Jaksa
J. Michael Kittross
Edmund B. Lambeth
Jeffrey Marks
Donald L. McBride
John Merrill
Robert Picard
Robert Roberts
Theodore Romberg
Glen Snowden
Robert Schmuhl
Christopher Sterling

FOREWORD

Squire Rushnell

A book about broadcasting and ethics should have great value in setting boundaries for anyone who embarks upon a broadcasting career. Certainly if you read or watch only the popular mass media--newspapers, television, radio, and magazines--you will be poorly prepared to become a network professional. A reference book on broadcast ethics gives the aspiring broadcaster the right guidelines to shoot for and presents a wide scope of literature about positive role models to emulate.

This reference is a good source book that can raise the reader's awareness of the vast number of books and publications about ethical questions in the industry. If you were to ask me to name five books about broadcasting ethics, I would probably have to think about it a little bit. Yet I know that there are a great many out there that do not come immediately to mind. it seems to me that a road map to all the sources is a valuable tool for any broadcaster who is constantly attempting to review his options.

Recently I received a letter from a lady who said she had been commissioned to write a book about Jessica Savitch, that wonderful newscaster at NBC who was tragically killed when her car crashed into the

Delaware River. I had felt very sad about that because I had admired her a lot since my "Good Morning America" days, when I often thought that she would be a terrific morning communicator for us. The woman in her letter said she wanted to interview me for her book, but her invitation puzzled me because I had no memory of having met Savitch. The letter said that in her autobiography Savitch noted that I had once interviewed her when I was young and working in Boston, and she had just completed college. Of course, I did not remember her because she was only another of the many young people I tried to spend time with and give guidance, too.

So I wrote to the woman and told her that I was sorry, but that I didn't know how to help her since I had never met Jessica Savitch. However, it turned out that my secretary had been reading the Savitch autobiography also, and, much to my surprise, it did indeed mention that the first person who had given Savitch an interview was this young man at Boston's WBZ-TV, Squire Rushnell. He did not offer her a job, but he *was* the first employer to take her seriously and offer encouragement.

I choked up as I read. To think that I had met a person who later so impressed me, but I had no awareness that I had had any impact on her life. It seems to me that a compilation of bibliographic sources and materials about this industry can serve as a valuable reminder for those of us too busy to reflect upon the most significant moments, people, and ethical decisions in our own history.

Moreover, we are always trying to find better ways to understand the public. Certainly those of us who have failed many times in this business have done so because we were not listening to what the audiences and trends were saying to us, or we were not seeing clearly. That is another reason we need to be open to all forms of feedback about our practices and programming--it heightens our sensitivity to the people we serve. One cannot merely pursue Neilsen studies and last week's programming numbers and make arbitrary judgments. One *must* dig much deeper and be aware of *people*. Often ethical dilemmas begin when people and relevant human factors are overlooked.

Also the implications of research can be tremendously important: reading what sociologists have said about the baby boomers returning to traditional values for example, has had a profound impact upon my programming for children during the past five years. These ideas came from some academic source or research record and *I do not even know now where it is*. Keeping track of research, data, and history is important, but it is extremely difficult without well-organized reference books.

Recently I was responsible for a children's television special called "The Kingdom Chums." The program did not receive a high national rating the next day. A full eight weeks later I received a report card on the actual program demographics and discovered that while "The Kingdom Chums" had not received high *household* ratings, during the last week of November it was the most popular program *among children* in all of television. The second most popular was "The Cosby Show" and third was "Family Ties." Number one with *that group* was "The Kingdom Chums."

That kind of *more discriminating* additional data, which I note is included in many of the studies this book lists, gives us much greater clarity about our approach to television. We understand our public better and can make more informed decisions. There is also an ethical dimension to deciding whether children's programming should be deemed successful *only* if it receives high ratings or if, on the other hand, it is genuinely rewarding to children.

Finally, case studies or histories are actually human *experience*. Those of us who have gone through the experience have firsthand knowledge and can avoid falling into the same traps (like those recorded in broadcast history) quite as easily. I find that these factors stemming from previous experience govern me every day of the year.

Recently, when I was sitting in my office, my television set had been turned to an independent station and I found myself for the first time in ten years watching "Leave It to Beaver," a program that certainly had a major impact upon the baby boomers during their childhoods. It occurred to me that the reason the show was so successful was that it said something of meaning to American families. The audience knew how each character was going to respond to a particular situation. That kind of relationship with its audience holds true for all popular shows. The common denominator among successful television programs is character, whether it is Ted Knight as the arrogant newsman in "The Mary Tyler Moore Show" or Hawkeye in "M*A*S*H" or Archie Bunker in "All in the Family" the personalities in "St. Elsewhere" or "L.A. Law" or "Bugs Bunny" or "The Carebears." It is only with time that we develop the perspective to note such patterns--that characters win audiences to consistent viewing of particular programs. A historical perspective brings clarity to the hidden structures in television's relationship to society.

So I am pleased to find a work that leads one to histories of important broadcasting cases and valuable research, and that is a standards and practices guide simultaneously. Potentially a bibliography of this scope will be useful for my colleagues, the public, scholars, advertisers, and competitors.

Perhaps it is an ethical responsibility for those of us within the industry to be more sensitive to our public and for our public in turn to be better informed about the moral choices we constantly face within the industry. This book serves both functions and introduces the student to our controversial but rewarding activities and programming. For all of us this work provides an opportunity to be more personally responsible, a challenge that begins with being better informed.

Squire Rushnell
ABC-TV, Vice President
Late Night and Children's Television

PREFACE

Clifford G. Christians

My son became sixteen years old this summer and within days received his driver's license. Having his own car keys was an unmistakable sign of maturity. We have delighted in his growth ever since. *Television and Ethics* brought vivid memories of the keys. What an obvious symbol of growth in communication ethics! The book is a visible marker by which historians will catalog the field's progress.

This reference text brings to mind another experience, one disconnected from and unrelated to the keys in content. Mary Tyler Moore's "Incredible Dream" was a spectacular television special, an ostentatious but impressive critique of human history. Remember the hand toward the finale, emerging from the ancient source of all life, the sea? Fashioned of foam rubber, the white hand wafts Ben Vereen, Moore, and the Manhattan Transfer to shore while Mary sings "Morning Has Broken." This bibliography likewise surfaces as a rubber raft carrying us to shore where life can move forward in earnest.

Am I too romantic? Perhaps. Books of this sort are made in the trenches. Their authors dig to bedrock, leaving as the proverb goes, "no stone unturned," and then chop and cut until only the redeemable is left. But for all that, Emerson College ought to be celebrated for hosting the first national Conference on Television and Ethics and sponsoring this resulting book. *Television and Ethics* represents an occasion that ought not to go unrecognized while we busily work its pages for help with our research and teaching.

The Greeks distinguish two kinds of time-*chronos* (everyday sequence of events) and *chairos* (moments of opportunity, of unusual potential). These are *chairos* days in communication ethics. An observer feels like the Hebrew prophet Ezekiel who once saw a stirring in the mulberry trees and dead bones coming to life. Interest is burgeoning everywhere. Mass media ethics is a growth industry. Conventions include ethics programs regularly, and the Speech Communication Association recently made ethics its entire convention theme. Seventy-five or more courses in media ethics have been initiated since 1980 in American colleges and universities, 300 percent more than the five previous years.

The Gannett, Poynter, and Markle foundations and the American Society of Newspaper Editors are funding research and curriculum development in ethics. Several new books have entered the market recently, and another eight or nine are in progress. Late in 1985 Brigham Young University launched the *Journal of Mass Media Ethics*. A recent doctoral dissertation at Harvard examined ethics instruction in journalism schools. Organizations such as the Association for Responsible Communication have emerged and others such as the Radio and Television News Directors Association and the Society of Professional Journalists/SDX maintain national ethics committees.

Carping from members of the public continues. And no media institutions are exempt--the press, entertainment television, theater advertising, and public relations. "Cynical, unfair, mindless, exploitative, incompetent, power hungry"--the criticism floods in from several quarters and television usually suffers the most. As the *Christian Science Monitor* recently noted: "The medium is widely pictured as a runaway, money driven machine without a heart--pumping out lowest-common-denominator programming at the behest of the highest bidder."

At the 1984 Emerson Conference on Television and Ethics, Norman Lear charged that television is inspired only by the cult of large audiences: "Television's moral North Star is quite simply, How do I win Tuesday night at 8?" At times the unthinking crowd even demands censorship.

But the condemnations are yielding a modest dividend. Never before have the mass media become so aware of their need for responsibility. I hear of stimulating debate in the newsroom about the invasion of privacy, compassion, promises of confidentiality, and the press's role in social justice. Some television producers struggle with moral dilemmas regarding violence and a consumption economy. Advertising and public relations, here and there, seek to distinguish legitimate persuasion from coercion and manipulation.

The sparks and glimmers, however, must still be fanned into open flame. There is decided movement, but much goes laterally or in circles rather than down to the core, the square root. There are more debates today, certainly--and research, slogans, and posturing, even a raised consciousness--but no quantum leap in quality, substance, integrity, or universality.

At this opportune time, we need more evidence of the systematic work the editors have demonstrated preparing this bibliography. Progress over the long term, I believe, depends upon our producing a sturdy ethical substructure. While we cope with the ongoing rush of events, profit-making, and political realities, educators and professionals who care must be challenged to contribute their minds and beings to unglamorous foundation building.

Much of the material cataloged in this volume enables us to broaden our range of ethical inquiry. As we probe its documents we will gain facility in examining substantive issues toward greater insight. Keeping our eyes upon this material rather than upon modern predicaments will orient us in fruitful directions. Professor Cooper concludes in the introduction that the television and ethics literature, while abundant, is impoverished. It is my hope that publication of this book will prevent endless duplication; instead of reinventing the wheel, we can build upon the accomplishments to date toward more definitive statements.

Walter Lippmann is considered America's greatest twentieth-century journalist, or is it Edward R. Murrow? For my purpose here, Lippmann's legacy best illustrates my call to serious workmanship. When faced in the 1920's with moral skepticism, collapsing standards, and angry assaults similar to the situation today, Lippmann responded with *A Preface to Morals*, which was far from irrelevant or bizarre. It became a best-seller (six printings the first year) and a rallying point for broad exploration into the despair of his time. Lippmann taught us the value of being a scholar in a troubled world who never let the dilemmas tear him loose from the principal domain beneath the turbulent surface.

It is always an academic's delight to turn from our haphazard attempts at information gathering and feast upon a full larder stocked neatly floor to ceiling. I took it as a personal challenge to locate one source or technique or strategy that the authors overlooked. I came up empty-handed myself and pass along the same challenge to every reader. A second edition would benefit enormously from additional citations not yet discovered.

Meanwhile, our good intentions and high energy may continue to be frustrated by the nomenclature. The introduction and methodology sections summarize methodological problems accurately. The manner in which the editors confront terminology strikes me as enlightened. They make the right choices regarding boundaries, in my view, including and excluding citations in reasonable ways.

Ethics, morals, and *values* and their cognates, have proved particularly troublesome and the introduction correctly begins by sifting through them. In compiling references, the authors could not ignore conventions, lapses, and confusions in the literature to date. Even specialists in philosophy cannot always agree on definitions, so why should nonphilosophers be expected to use them uniformly in a set of articles gathered from all over the world?

Nonetheless, I cherish the dream that as further editions of *Television and Ethics* are compiled, the literature represented not only will improve in quality but will demonstrate at least a minimal standardization of terms. Therefore, allow me the pedantry here of reiterating definitions that, in some form, might aid us in organizing our future ideas more circumspectly. On the one hand, with nuclear war, racism, terrorism, and injustice on the international agenda, life is too urgent for quibbling about abstract words. On the other, I will highlight such words, on the basis of the ancient wisdom that only fools refuse to remove a grain of sand from their shoes, believing they are called to more noble tasks.

It would assist the bibliographer and perceptibly sharpen our discourse if we henceforth utilize the definitions outlined in the introduction--*ethics* as the systematic study of principles that underlie human behavior, *morals* as our actual codes of conduct, and *values* as those entities or mental attitudes considered good or desirable.

Definitions also remind me to promote a certain kind of ethics as particularly valuable at present. The disciplinary inquiries that appear in the bibliography regarding news or entertainment can be classified into six types:

Applied: Ethics concerned with norms in terms of their relationship to human situations where dilemmas occur.

Metaethics: The philosophical study of ethical theories, the status of moral claims, and the nature of the good and right.

Normative: Ethics that fuses principles with actual morality so that principal judgments emerge about classes of conduct and states of affairs.

Descriptive: Ethics that reports on how ethical decision making functions in a given culture.

Social: Ethics in the social philosophy tradition where society and institutions are critiqued holistically and structurally.

Individualistic: Ethical approaches that focus essentially on practitioners' quandaries and presume that solutions inhere in the right actions of persons counted one by one.

Notice that these approaches to ethics are deliberately organized in pairs, to recommend the first of each pair (1, 3, 5) instead of the second (2, 4, 6). The compilation in this volume raises the water level. As we work from it, I recommend that our media ethics be applied, normative, and social in character. In fact, if we understand the word *normative* correctly, that label is sufficient by itself. The challenge at present is not merely to engage in more ethical inquiry of whatever sort but rather to inspire normative ethics. The conundrums in our culture necessitate a more enlightened mass media ethics than on that essentially presumes the status quo.

Normative theory rooted in social ethics indicates what ought to be done; that is, it articulates a relationship between television and society founded upon principles. This normative theory sets a direction, provides an alternative framework for formulating policy and writing scripts, and provides protection against cooptation. In Arthur Dyck's terms, normative ethics equips us to discover how best to proceed; before we act we learn to do so with imagination and intelligence. The books listed in this volume may give us greater cognizance of these choices and of our options.

This book represents an achievement, since for whatever reasons the inspection of television and entertainment have languished in the larger domain of media ethics. Newspapers and reporting have attracted the best ethical thinking to date, although in this information age television is our most powerful arbiter of cultural values. While helping to rectify this imbalance, if *Television and Ethics* also inspires normative theory, the entire field of communication ethics will be permanently enriched.

Clifford G. Christians
University of Illinois--Urbana

INTRODUCTION

Thomas W. Cooper

This bibliography is designed to assist readers and researchers interested in the relationships between television and ethics. There are more appropriate bibliographies for readers interested in *either* television *or* ethics, or those interested in mass communication or philosophy, although selected entries from each of those fields are included here. In this bibliography we have selected books, articles, speeches, and theses that treat the ethical dimensions of television *programs* and *practices*.

Literature regarding ethical issues *portrayed by* television (that is televised lectures about philosophical ethics, documentaries about business or medical ethics, entertainment programs using ethical issues for plot tension) is a much narrower subject, and is not the focus of this volume. Thus television and ethics means the ethical issues surrounding television's influence and existence, not televised ethics.

Definitions

Herein *television* is defined more broadly than mere invention, entertainment source, or information straw. The systems that connect sets, audiences, and in many cases advertisers are called business or industry in many countries, and institutions or governments in others. Thus much of our survey considers the social sciences as well as the humanities from an academic standpoint; from a professional perspective we focus upon trade journals as well as popular magazines.

Television, both as technology and information conduit, was born into a large family: parents and in-laws such as journalism, broadcasting, government regulation, the performing arts, and (in some countries) advertising as much shape the field as surround it. Television continues to both contribute to and reflect change within such areas, as well as the social sciences of politics, economics, sociology, and psychology. Consequently, *television* is broadly defined to include the contextual factors that organize its structures and attitudes.

In public conversation *ethics* is intended to mean moral problems or individual choices between competing value systems. Within this bibliography, however, three definitions are included within our overview of *ethics*, as in Paul Edward's *Dictionary of Philosophy*, vol. 5 (New York: Macmillan Co., 1967):

1. A general pattern or a way of life.
2. A set of rules or code of conduct or responsibility.
3. *Inquiry about* ways of life (no. 1) or codes of responsibility (no. 2).

Some serious scholars of philosophy are more likely to equate definitions 1 or 2 with "morals" and reserve 3 for "ethics." Many television professionals and their publics use and may confuse all three. Clifford Christians's excellent list of six definitions of the subsets of ethics is particularly helpful in avoiding such confusion (see Preface).

Included here are texts that treat one, two, or all *levels* of the definition. For example, television can appear to hold or teach general behavior patterns or a way or ways of life and thus transmit ethics. Second, specific national and professional codes of responsibility, standards, and conduct have generated a large literature about censorship, regulation, and several questions of responsibility: Who is responsible? To whom are they responsible? What is responsibility? Finally, the study of (cf. *inquiry about*) such patterns, codes, and behavior has spawned a new subdiscipline within university curricula entitled "media ethics." Communication ethics, journalism ethics, broadcasting ethics, and similar fields have been tributaries of this larger river.

Values, a term frequently but erroneously equated with ethics (see Clifford Christians's Preface), is central to the relationship between ethics and television. Values and ethics are not interchangeable but are closely related. For example: values *may* be viewed as the pillars upon which ethical pediments rest. Given this image, only when these pillars (values) are shaken (threatened) are ethical systems also unsteady. At such times, ethics attracts the attention of writers and researchers. Universally encultured, revered, and upheld values, and the ethical systems that preserve them, foster little debate or interest.

Thus, a literature of ethics may well flower in atmospheres of conflicting, contending, and changing values. Such changes and conflicts during the second half of this century--artificial versus natural, mainstream versus minority, media versus government, Marxism versus capitalism, countercultural versus establishment, chauvinist versus feminist, the "public interest" versus the public's interests, network conservatism versus cable opportunism, broadcasting versus narrowcasting, lowest common denominator versus highest common purpose, public versus commercial, libertarian versus authoritarian--these forces and their related value systems have created the tensions from which ethical choices and debates flourish.

Hence, literature treating values is relevant, but relevant only to the extent that it has direct bearing upon the practices and programming of television. Moreover, eras of transformation, whether epitomized by "Watergate" or "Irangate," bring much ethical emphasis quickly to the fore of public attention.

Furthermore, governments favoring regulation or deregulation of media control arise in response to the modern social, economic, and political forces listed above. Such governments may appoint, nullify, empower, or stunt commissions, courts, legislation, and agencies that originate and enforce legal policy. Ethical and legal concerns of virtually all eras and cultures are inextricably intertwined. So, too, are the literatures of media ethics and media law.

Scope

Although many *general* texts about mass media, ethics, television, journalism, and so on, are included within this reference book, they are like the bordering strips of territory that surround a country on a national map--they provide a sense of context and continuity within the large mosaic of disciplines, but are peripheral to the focus of attention. Such general works seem to locate and circumscribe the field and to some degree explain its premises, yet they lack the depth, specificity, and documentation of works that primarily focus upon television and ethics. Hence, general values are peripheral to this study and are only representatively included, but discussions of values that illuminate the nature of ethical debates about television densely populate this body of literature.

Entries that are marginal to television and ethics (for example, works about business ethics, medical ethics, history of broadcasting, general ethics since Socrates and Plato) are fewer in number than the primary body of works that discuss television and ethics specifically. Marginal works are included to help readers and researchers who are comparative (do media professionals handle conflict of interest differently from doctors and lawyers?), contextual (where does this field fit on the map of knowledge?), and curious (how did we get here or where do we go from here?). Moreover, even to the specialist, such works help make sense of isolated topics and case studies, whether historically, politically, or philosophically.

Criteria for Selection

Two guiding criteria for selection, relevance and substance, outweigh by far two secondary criteria, recency and perspective. A highly substantial but dated text might be far more useful than a current, but largely irrelevant one. On the other hand, where many works adequately describe a perennial debate, those with more current case studies and methodology are more likely to prove useful. It seemed more valuable to include, rather than exclude, borderline cases, and let the reader provide further criteria for his or her own selection.

Humility is the natural by-product of editing bibliographies. Few bibliography editors can claim to have thoroughly read all the books listed within their own catalog, let alone all those that might be included within an international, multidecade search. All the abstracts in this bibliography have been inspected and, in most cases, compressed and rewritten for continuity. But many titles remain *only* titles and represent works we have skimmed or in a few cases never seen. In similar fashion, although selection is a highly disciplined process, involving feedback from leading scholars in the field, ultimately such work includes subjective factors and collective predilections. Three other research teams may have chosen slightly or even vastly different entries. For this reason we encourage readers to mail in entries (complete titles, authors, cities of publication, publishers, and dates) they feel were unnecessarily omitted, so we may incorporate as much as is appropriate in future editions.

Research methodologist Robert Sullivan delineates below our primary means of collecting titles: (1) computer data base searches, (2) manual compilation of printed abstracts, (3) scanning of book reviews and abstract anthologies, (4) assimilation by correspondence of reading lists, bibliographies, and reference lists compiled by other, and (5) the assembly of a team of advising editors who magnified our search for "black holes" or glaring omissions.

Drawing the Line

At every stage of development, team members have been faced with questions about the boundaries of television and ethics. As and example, at first glance all works relating to the *regulation* of broadcasting seem central to the domain. Certainly at the point where regulation is a specific response to the violation of ethical codes, it is inextricably tied to the literature of media ethics. But where books and essays focus more upon the blanket history of radio broadcast regulation, upon influential personalities, upon technology, upon the form and not the substance of legislative bureaucracies, they become one step removed from this discussion. Many other subject areas are "neighbors" which we include representatively but not thoroughly.

Titles often deceive. An excellent chapter about an important ethical issue may be discovered in a book within a distant field. Conversely, every book that has a title suggestive of television and ethics is not always accurately or literally titled and may wander from its topic. Furthermore, the word *ethics* is often misused or, if correctly used, may be hidden in a table of contents or index. Many of those books listed in "communication ethics" or "journalism ethics" make *no* mention of ethics within the table of contents but are germane.

Three Audiences

This work is intended as a companion to the public and the television professional, as much as to the academic. Moreover, even from a strictly academic standpoint, the question the editor faces is not "how academic is this book?" but rather "how *useful* could this work be to a discriminating academic?" The editing of this bibliography has filtered out many peripheral texts, but the researcher must provide a finer filter depending upon his audience and subject. Thus, although scholarly standards are foremost, we also intend to serve the professional and the public.

Hence, a balance among general, academic, professional, and trade publications has been sought. One finding, however, is that such a balance does not exist naturally within the field. Critics, academics, and other "outsiders" (concerned politicians, parents, and organizations) often are more vocal about ethical concerns that are television professionals, if published articles are representative. Consequently, the small proportion of titles from trade and industry journals represents an imbalance discovered during our searches.

Defining Categories and the Table of Contents

In establishing the boundaries of the work we first deleted numerous entires to narrow the immense volume of material. The editor could have easily listed two volumes of citations, but the book would have lost specificity and penetration.

Moreover, many entries could have been cross-listed within different categories and originally over 60 percent of the entries appeared in two or more categories. However, to avoid excessive duplication, less than 5 percent of all titles are now listed in more than one category. If a work seemed to focus on two subjects *throughout* its text, it became a *candidate* for double listing and may have actually been entered with slightly *different* abstracts so as to emphasize categories.

As with all categories, these contain areas of overlap and some measure of arbitrary choice. On the other hand, they are intended to help the reader quickly find the most pertinent sources in his or her search.

Introduction

Many authors prefer to write about the somewhat large fields of mass media ethics, journalism ethics, or communication ethics rather than a single medium such as television. Some of the most rigorous and penetrating writing about television, conversely, is found in works of sociology, psychology, education, economics, and journalism. Robert Sullivan will describe this mosaic of "homes" for television literature in his essay on methodology.

Abstracts

Abstracts accompany 473 out of 1,170 titles. We discovered that existing abstracts varied in length from one sentence to a short essay. Consequently, to provide greater symmetry, a digestible guide for readers, and essential knowledge, many abstracts have been abridged and paraphrased. Sentences and paragraphs that describe portions of a book or article least related to television and ethics were easiest to eliminate. Other sentences and paragraphs were deleted, not because they were unimportant, but because they were not essential to the primary theme. Some abstracts are exceedingly threadbare such as the one-sentence subtitle phrases used by *Columbia Journalism Review*.

Virtually all abstracts are reprinted by permission of the author, a data base service, the editor, or an anthology of abstracts. Their final shape derived more from the criteria of substance and simplicity than from secondary criteria, symmetry and style. Readers are encouraged to submit additional abstracts to be reviewed and edited for future editions.

At the conclusion of each abstract, authorship and editing are ascribed in chronological order of the writing and adaptation of each abstract. For example, if the original abstract submitted by the author was ideal for this bibliography, the citation conclusion of the abstract reads <AU>, "author." If, however, the *Journal of Dissertation Abstracts in Journalism and Mass Communication* (fictitious title) edited the author's abstract, which was rewritten by us for this bibliography, the final citation conclusion would read "author/JODAJMC/editor," or in our abbreviated terms <AU/JOD/ED>.

Some of the many abbreviations at the end of abstracts are initials of contributors such as DLM (Donald L. McBride), DE (Deni Elliott), or CC (Clifford Christians). The vast majority of abstracts have been written or rewritten by Thomas Cooper and are attributed to <ED>.

Findings

Although some of our findings are methodological and thus discussed within Robert Sullivan's following essay, our research has led to many thought about the content, scope, and status of the literature within the new field of television ethics. A few of our primary observations follow:

1. Works on television and ethics, although an enormous field, make up an impoverished literature. Given the documented impact of television on human behavior, cognition, and attitudes, far fewer substantial works exist than might be reasonably anticipated. The 1,170 entries listed here, selected from more than 2,500 candidates, represent many attempts to find tools and terms for a proper discussion of the subject. Several entries are marginal to the field, and others borrow from larger categories--broadcasting, communication, values, and philosophy.

2. Much of the discussion of television and ethics is unsystematic opinion. We have excluded many such essays--from newspaper editorials to many articles in *TV Guide* and similar magazines since, as Harold Innis stated, "opinion is the lowest form of wisdom." Although we could not systematically screen all books that are in some way inaccurate, it was easier to screen many works that do not appear to *strive* for accuracy, such as those that are not documented, qualified, nor logically developed. Serious documented *research* surrounding the *ethics* of television is much less pervasive than homespun commentary about television as a perceived good or evil.

3. Particularly barren of commentary are journals published by the broadcasting industry and its supporting agencies and services. If ethics is narrowly interpreted to mean moral criticism, one is not surprised to discover a lack of published commentary within any industry. Moral *self-criticism* is seldom published within large corporations, particularly within publications that serve as a form of public relations or advertising. On the other hand, ethics is far more than *moral criticism*--ethics can include a system of thinking, a menu of behavioral options, a description of standards and practices, and a choice between merely human and humane conditions. For those within the television industry to frequently eliminate themselves from this sizable discussion and literature is more than noteworthy--it is revealing. Those industry journals that have included *some* ethical discussion (such as *Comment, Television Quarterly,* the *Communicator*) are not readily available

to the general public nor even to scholars through major periodical guides and mainstream data bases.

4. Possibly the most substantial quantitative research has been conducted within the province of television and values, rather than within television and ethics. Perhaps the categories themselves, "ethics" and "values", imply differing degrees of measurable phenomena. Although both terms may describe phenomena that are either vague or specific, values *seem* more specific, more concrete, and thus more conducive to measurement. Although values are themselves slippery intangibles, value categories seem more constant and simple than ethics, which may imply relative frames of reference and increased complexity (systems). Moreover, measuring ethics may make as much sense as measuring cybernetics or metaphysics, whereas measuring *values* is more *credible*, if equally difficult.

5. A growth in attempted measurement, particularly of value (attitude) *change*, as associated with television viewing and content, is reflected in the increase of attitude studies, dissertations, and books written within the past twenty years. Studies of particular television programs "All in the Family", channels (MTV, Playboy) and audiences (blacks, females) are far more commonplace, whereas studies organized by issue or subject (for example, invasion of privacy, censorship, source concealment, fabricated docudrama) are still relatively few. Within the larger field of mass communication literature, studies of behavioral change, attitude formation, and value modification have been placed within the larger category of television "effects." We have followed that system of categorization within our table of contents.

6. Historically, the study of media ethics has broadened from the original field of journalism ethics. Professionally, the field has borrowed from professional quarters such as medical ethics, business ethics, and legal ethics. Nevertheless, it is much rarer to find a book on professional ethics with a section on television ethics than to find a text on journalism ethics with a section on television or broadcasting. Despite the many contexts that frame television and ethics (for example, mass entertainment, philosophy of culture, communication standards, and popular morality), the field is increasingly seen within the domain of "media ethics" and as an extension of "journalism ethics." Some texts focus upon mass communication or journalism ethics as their universe and make television, like radio and newspapers, a separate category. But over 50 percent of all texts listed subdivide media ethics by issue categories (sources, invasion of privacy, censorship) and choose examples on a case-by-case method without regard to medium. In such

frequent cases, television becomes background and the type of ethical dilemma becomes dominant.

7. Possibly there is an inverse correlation between the *scope* of an ethical question and the scope of literature that surrounds it. For example, the most basic and profound questions--Is television's presence in society ethical? Which ethical systems are transmitted by television?--have attracted a much smaller literature than smaller subtopics within television ethics: What are the effects of specific programming--Children's television? Violent genres? Erotic episodes? How accurately are blacks portrayed by television? Women? Consumer products?

8. There is relatively little questioning of four fundamental characteristics of television. Most observation calls for a questioning of television's content or impact, but very little presses on to challenge its (a) presence, (b) purpose, (c) language, and (d) ubiquity. Those few works that consider the elimination or restructuring of television are vastly outnumbered by those that recommend milder changes in regulation, programming, advertising, and accuracy. The body of reasoned commentary surrounding theater, from Aristotle to Esslin, or of film, from Eisenstein to Metz, has no equivalent serious development of an ethics, aesthetics, or epistemology of television. Little penetrating thought seems to proceed backward from observation of specific television content to essential questions about the nature, purpose, and role of television. Ethics is useful only as such basic questions are clarified, challenged, and answered.

9. Since the 1960s, most research about the *effects* of mass communication has focused upon television. Corresponding ethical examination of the conclusions of effects research has been much higher in television than other mass media. Nevertheless, within this more clinical literature, ethical examination of effects is itself much smaller than the body of effects research. Ethical interpretation of empirical research is neither comprehensive nor systematic. A synthesis of those studies listed within this bibliography alone could provide a plethora of data for the examination of several differing larger questions about the fundamental *nature* of television's use, potential, health, and overall influence. Like this bibliography, television research and its *ethical* interpretation are still embryonic.

Introduction

Acknowledgments

Many of those who shared their own research we have named contributing editors, and those who have analyzed the original text for mistakes, oversights, and overall balance we distinguish as advising editors. We are grateful to acknowledge Glen Snowden, Eric Elbot, Clifford Christians, John Michael Kittross, and others listed earlier for their contributions and Christopher Sterling, Bob Roberts, Donald McBride, Eugene Goodwin, and Clifford Christians for excellent advice. The central core team that has worked conscientiously on this text for over a year is comprised of research methodologist Robert Sullivan, business manager/publisher Chris Weir, and during 1985-1986 programmer/search director Peter Medaglia. All these people have contributed ideas, insight, and interest far beyond their special skills and are very much, in many ways, co-editors. Cooper and Weir began the project, but all four worked closely together for many months in a fluid team effort. Dr. David Maxwell gave generous support to the initial idea by Cooper.

President Allen Koenig of Emerson College, by initiating the national conference on Television and Ethics in 1984, provided much backing and stimulus to this work. John Sawhill, president, and Leo Palmer, executive director of the National Academy of Television Arts and Sciences, New England chapter, provided strong support for the conference and affiliated activities. Many of those included within that conference--Norman Lear, William Sloane Coffin, Morton Dean, and Fran Plude--were among those who built a foundation upon which such a symposium may move forward. The second conference in 1987--highlighted by the presence of Fred Friendly, Ed Hume, and the leadership of Clifford Curley, Skip Sikora, and especially Chris Weir--expanded that emphasis and momentum.

The Provost of Emerson College at the time our spadework was being done was John Michael Kittross who offered immeasurably sound advice and talented editing. His successor, Dean Jacqueline Liebergott, sustains a strong commitment to ethics research and provides many levels of invaluable support.

Numerous hands have combed many libraries during this process. Kerry Howland, Wendy Lerner, Randi Chudnow, Eithne Johnson, and Michelle Skittino are among the patient assistants who helped find obscure dates, editions, and sundry details. Our wives, Nancy Cooper, Nancie Weir, and Lisa Sullivan, have patiently supported much burning of the midnight oil and extra meetings. Kittross's and Liebergott's team of assistants--Brian McCarthy, Sally Arnold, Pam Roy, and Mary Ellen Horne--helped in every way possible.

Special thanks are given to Gerd Bond, Bill Gilligan, Debra Whitmoyer, and the Boston Computer Society for advice and support. Donna Donnelly's keyboard expertise saved many wasted hours during the home stretch. Finally, Julie McAdoo provided useful and polished indexes.

Among the "family" of those studying media ethics are many special friends who inspire and act as mentors for each other's works. Although all the contributing and advising editors are such people, particular mention should be made of other academics such as John Merrill, Robert Hilliard, Jay Black, David Gordon, Ralph Barney, Sissela Bok, and Chuck Culver who may be counted on as a consistent support group for those committed to the field and to quality education. Moreover, many professionals also *stand for,* rather than merely mention, ethics--Squire Rushnell, Willard Scott, Dennis Weaver, Tom Goodgame, Skip Sikora, Diane Willis, Chris Conongla, and many others. Entire organizations such as the Association for Responsible Communication and the *Journal of Mass Media Ethics* provide an increased anchoring for research of this nature. Our genuine appreciation is extended to all.

This bibliography is the outcome of constant teamwork. To all parts of the team--Emerson College, its Divisions of Mass Communication and Continuing Education, and their leadership--we are most thankful. Finally, many decisions, after the excellent input of Chris, Bob, and in earlier months, Peter, were left with one person and final policies, after wise advice from Cliff, Mike, and others, were left with the same person. Despite the formidable contributions of many, most of the eleventh-hour work inevitably was inherited by one person. In that spirit I give full credit to the team, but take full responsibility for the work's editorial policy, scope, format, final contents, and any shortcomings thereof.

This book owes much to the spirit of Emerson College, its faculty, administration, students, staff, founder (Charles Wesley Emerson), and the latter's cousin (Ralph Waldo Emerson), who considered books among his most stimulating companions. A bibliography is a portable library of such books. It is our longing that such a library leads others not only to useful references and little-known works of importance but to the people and passions behind them.

Dr. Thomas W. Cooper
Emerson College

METHODOLOGY

Robert Sullivan

The organized study of television faces dilemmas that make access to important literature difficult for scholars, for students, and especially for interested laypersons. Most of these problems stem from the multidisciplinary nature of the field of communications studies.

To a large extent the primary literature of the fields of communication and television studies has been fractured into subsets of the literatures of the formal social sciences. This literature is seen and treated as a discrete component of each of these formal sciences--psychology, sociology, education, anthropology, history, political science, and others. Thus, any attempt to access formal literature on communication effects and processes takes a searcher on a voyage through the vagaries of viewpoint and assessment technique of such disparate sources as *Sociological Abstracts, Social Sciences Index, ERIC, Psychological Abstracts*, and *Social Science Citation Index.*

The situation for the researcher becomes worse when the literature sought is not of a formal nature but of that nebulous designation, humanistic. *The Reader's Guide to Periodical Literature* (and its imitators), *Dissertation Abstracts, Humanities Index, Topicator, Arts and Humanities Citation Index,*

Access, and *Business Periodicals Index* provide widely varying points of access to humanist, secondary, or popular literature on television studies.

The only indexing service available that attempts to capture the cross-disciplinary literature of media studies is *Communication Abstracts*. Without this invaluable tool librarians and researchers would be virtually lost during major projects.

A more serious problem exists for the researcher who examines the field of television, however. As Tom Cooper points out in "The Movement toward Depth," (*Przekazy: opinie [Messages and opinions]*(Warsaw), forthcoming 1988), the number of research instruments examining the mass media is inadequate relative to the impact of these communication technologies on our lives and our society.

The researcher, then, must contend with two basic scholarly problems: first, that the literature on television is, in general, inadequate to his or her purposes, and second, that bibliographic access is scattered and incomplete.

The Method

This bibliography was compiled as a resource for the conferences on Television and Ethics that were co-sponsored by Emerson College and the New England chapter of the National Academy of Television Arts and Sciences in December 1984 and March 1987. This volume will provide access to the literature examining the topics covered by the conferences for the public, the professional, and the scholar.

The bibliography was compiled in a four-step process. First, a series of on-line searches were completed. *ERIC, Psychological Abstracts, Sociological Abstracts*, and *ABI/Inform* were examined using a set of descriptor commands that yielded a compact, relevant set of citations primarily from academic texts, primary journals, and monographs. The combination of terms used corresponded to the phrase "television and (ethics or values)"; the abstracts provided by these citations were used as a basis for a precis of their conclusions.

The second component of the bibliography is the result of the solicitation, by Dr. Cooper, of course reading lists and bibliographies from a team of scholars and academics noted for their teaching of media studies. These included such scholars as Ed Lambeth from the University of Missouri, Glen Snowden , Eric Elbot and John M. Kittross from Emerson College, Clifford Christians of the University of Illinois at Urbana,

Christopher Sterling from George Washington University, Robert Roberts from Temple University's School of Communication and Theater, Donald McBride of the University of South Dakota, and Eugene Goodwin from Pennsylvania State University. The citations yielded by this process form the classical backbone of the study of ethical concerns and the media. We cannot thank these scholars enough for their generosity of effort, material, and time. The skill they brought to their evaluations of the literature of the field is greatly appreciated. This material was consolidated by Dr. Cooper and Mr.Weir. Then additional material was independently collected by Dr. Cooper through research, supplementary correspondence, and detective work.

These three steps yielded a bibliography of material from primarily academic sources. To broaden our search to include more professional materials, other data bases were consulted, such as those published by the Information Access Corporation--*Magazine Index, Trade and Industry Index,* and *Legal Resources Index.* These then had to be reviewed for content and relevance, and selected for the bibliography.

The final stages of compilation were primarily manual and highly selective. A manual search through *Social Sciences Index* and *Humanities Index* was intended to ensure against any gaps in the academic portion of the bibliography resulting from reliance upon too rigid a set of descriptors in the on-line search. *Communication Abstracts* was also searched manually for relevant citations beyond the scope of the consulted on-line sources. Later, to ensure maximum comprehensiveness, hitherto uncovered citations were painstakingly retrieved through both on-line and manual sources.

The Results

The strategies above yielded well over 1,000 citations from which the editors have chosen over 650 for publication in this bibliography. Where they came from, how they were retrieved, and their assessed relevance to the topic should be instructive to both lay investigators and professional researchers.

1. On-line sources: Academic
As stated above the first set of citations was retrieved from four on-line indexes that compile bibliographies from scholarly sources: journals, dissertations, conference papers, and books. What follows is a list of these data bases, notes on their coverage and size, and counts of "hits" by individual

terms and strategy. All were later searched under additional author, title, and subject sets.

ERIC
1966-July 1986 (500,000+ records). The on-line version of both *Current Index to Journals in Education* and *Research in Education* (the indexing source for ERIC documents).

PSYCINFO
1 January 1967-31 December 1987 (500,000+ records). The on-line version of *Psychological Abstracts*.

ABI/INFORM
1 January 1971-31 December 1987 (275,000+ records). Abstracting service for business and management journals. There is no paper equivalent.

SOCIOLOGICAL ABSTRACTS
1 January 1963-31 December 1987 (150,000+ records). The on-line version of *Sociological Abstracts*.

ERIC
10,600 Television
2,648 Ethics
12,137 Values
198 Television and (Ethics or Values)

PSYCINFO
1,619 Television
1,559 Ethics
4,868 Values
23 Television and (Ethics or Values)

ABI/INFORM
2,845 Television
1,046 Ethics
797 Values
11 Television and (Ethics or Values)

SOCIOLOGICAL ABSTRACTS
1,100 Television
790 Ethics
2,324 Values
13 Television and (Ethics or Values)

The peculiarities of the ratios of subject material to citation base are expressed above. The rough count works out as follows:

Total Citations in Data Bases	Citations on Television	Television and Ethics or Values
> 1,500,000	> 16,000	< 250

It is instructive to note that these data bases, which analyze thousands of academic journals and monographs and number their citations in the millions, yielded approximately 250 citations on this topic. They were, however, closely relevant to our topic, and nearly 80 percent were included in the final compilation.

In addition to the sources mentioned above, the on-line versions of Philosopher's Index, Management Contents, Public Affairs Information Service (PAIS), Arts and Humanities Citation Index, and Religion Index were consulted. None of these indexes yielded significant numbers of citations on our topic that were not duplicates of material uncovered in other on-line and manual searches.

2. On-line sources: General

MAGAZINE INDEX 1959-87 (1,700,000+ records)
TRADE AND INDUSTRY INDEX 1981-87 (1,000,000+ records)
LEGAL RESOURCE INDEX 1980-87 (190,000+ records)

MAGAZINE INDEX
27,709 Television
4,877 Ethics
178 Values
217 Television and (Ethics or Values)

TRADE AND INDUSTRY INDEX
21,356 Television
1,903 Ethics
29 Values
106 Television and (Ethics or Values)

LEGAL RESOURCES INDEX
1,662 Television
3,169 Ethics
9 Values
20 Television and (Ethics or Values)

The ratio of hits to citation base is shown below.

Total Citations in Data Bases	Citations on Television	Television and Ethics or Values
>2,900,000	>50,000	350

It should be noted that most of the 355 citations retrieved from general readership on-line sources were, at best, marginally relevant to the purpose of the bibliography. Indeed, only about 50 citations out of the 350+ retrieved by the subject statement were included in the final compilation. The lack of depth of the popular literature on this topic is instructive and perhaps frightening; the lack of depth of indexing provided by the Information Access Corporation is evident and rather infuriating.

3. Manual searches: Indexes

Of all the paper indexes consulted, none was more relevant, encyclopedic, and practical than the H.W. Wilson Company's *Humanities Index*. It was searched from volume 1, 1973, through 1978 under all its "television. . ." listings and relevant "see also. . ." references. It yielded nearly 250 useful citations. There was almost no overlap between the citations retrieved from *Humanities Index* and those compiled from other sources, on-line or manual.

Similar searching in Wilson's *Social Sciences* Index, which was also searched from volume 1, 1973, yielded a much smaller set of relevant citations, almost all of which had been previously retrieved in the on-line searches of ERIC, Psycinfo, and SocAbs. This clearly supports the contention that the literature of the field of television and media studies is fractured and dispersed throughout the disciplines. Conversely, it can be argued that the indexers at *Psychological Abstracts* and *Sociological Abstracts* are undertaking a complete, disciplined, and thorough job of capturing the literature specific to their fields. Material, however, from source journals that support the humanities is often ignored, even if the material is built on the methodology of the hard social sciences and to a large extent supports those disciplines.

It should be noted that the H.W. Wilson Company, the publishers of both *Humanities Index* and *Social Sciences Index*, is in the process of making their products available in an on-line form called Wilsonline. The format was not available at the time this bibliography was compiled.

Other indexes were consulted for specific purposes. *Topicator* and portions of *Business Periodicals Index* (1973-86) were searched by subject for material on our topic. Little was retrieved that had not previously appeared as the result of other searches. *Communication Abstracts* was researched from volume 1, 1978, to 1986 for topical material and to establish title patterns by authors in the field.

4. Manual searches: Expert bibliographies

The fourth set of citations was made up of course reading lists and personally compiled bibliographies solicited from such widely respected authorities in the field of media studies as Christians, Snowden, McBride, Lambeth, Goodwin, and others. They responded generously, providing citations to nearly 400 books, book chapters, articles, and papers. Citations to books and book chapters in this bibliography come almost exclusively from these sources. The journal citations they provided served not only to expand our bibliography but to test our results from other sources for relevance and inclusiveness. Most of the abstracts were written or edited by Dr. Cooper. Incomplete or emphemeral citations were verified by myself.

One concern of all these scholars was made clear by the nature of the material submitted--that is, that any study of the specific effects of television or the mass media on American ethics or values must include a more general examination of the ethical base that is being effected. Included, therefore, with the citations directly germane to our topic were many citations from the classics in the field of ethical studies. We honor this commitment to the study of ethics with an 80-item bibliography on ethics and other contextual bibliographies (journalism ethics, professional ethics, communications ethics, and so on), which precede our more specific bibliography.

Conclusion

From the standpoint of methodology, this researcher leaves the reader with three strategic warnings about cross-disciplinary research in media studies.

1. There is little overlap between data bases or indexes on this subject: perhaps twenty citations were found to be duplicated among the on-line data bases. Neither is there significant overlap between the set of citations retrieved by search of the on-line sources concentrating in the social sciences and those citations found in *Humanities Index*. Citations found in *Social Sciences Index*, however, are likely also to be found in the interdisciplinary indexes, with abstracts and within a much larger citation base on this topic. All of this is to be expected. One would suggest that it is one more reflection of the fractured nature of media studies.

2. The disparities of indexing, specifically subject indexing, among indexes is a formidable problem. Researchers are well advised to exercise caution and patience when using multiple-concept strategies in multidisciplinary fields. The effectiveness of any search strategy varies greatly with use in different sources.

From the results listed above, it is obvious that *ethics, values,* and even *television* mean amazingly different things to different indexers. In each data base and index we combined our basic terms (television, ethics, values) with variant terms (broadcasting, mass media, media, morals, and so on) which we thought might have yielded similar sets of new citations. We found, however, that the basic index phrase (television and ethics or values) retrieved relevant citations most effectively. Judging by assessed relevance alone, citations from academic on-line sources provide far more sure retrieval than those compiled by the same strategy from more general sources. In print indexing, there is virtually no combined-concept subject terms that retrieve well in this field. Humanities Index was searched under the broadest possible subject heading, "Television." After this it was the same old slog.

3. One of the theses tested by this methodologist in this work was whether on-line sources available at the time could supply a relatively complete bibliography on a cross-disciplinary topic. On-line sources accounted for approximately 50 percent of the citations used in this volume. Although they captured a set of citations closely wedded to the concept of the bibliography, they were in no way complete. Manual searching was more than a compliment to the whole of this work. On-line searching is, at this point, simply too discipline-specific to produce cross-disciplinary bibliographies. Where there is no on-line disciplinary index, there is, obviously, no on-line bibliographic access.

As noted above, Humanities Index and Social Sciences Index have recently been made available in an on-line form as have other data bases such as Arts and Humanities Citation Index and Social Sciences Citation Index. It may well be that the arrival of these sources in on-line formats will change these conclusions in the future.

As enamored as we may become of the speed and depth of on-line indexing, the scholar's shoe-box index will never be replaced. The many scholars who donated their course lists and expert bibliographies provided us with more than the neutral result of a search command. They gave us tested products, assessed and used, and ordered in their quirky, individual, and evocative ways, and I thank them.

The building of bibliographic access to the literature of any academic discipline is endless. When that literature is as fractured and dispersed as that of formal communications studies, the process is complicated, to say the least. And when the problems of formal definition in such a field are translated into the language governing access to its literature, the scholar, the businessman, and most of all, the general public are poorly served indeed. We hope, by this bibliography, to address the needs of these constituencies in some small but serviceable way.

Robert Sullivan
Research Librarian
Emerson College

PERIODICALS MOST FREQUENTLY CITED

Periodical	Number of Articles Cited
Journal of Broadcasting	116
Journalism Quarterly	73
Journal of Communication	44
Columbia Journalism Review	30
Broadcasting	12
Quill	12
Etc.	12
Mass Comm Review	12
Journal of Mass Media Ethics	11
New York Times	11
Journal of Popular Culture	11
Variety	10
Indiana Law Journal	8
Communication	8
Newsweek	8
Communication Quarterly	8
Journal of Advertising	7
Time	7
Journalism Educator	6
Los Angeles Times	6

I. Ethical Contexts

I A. CLASSICAL ETHICS: PHILOSOPHY, THEOLOGY, AND SOCIOLOGY

1   ACKERMAN, B. Social Justice in the Liberal State. New Haven: Yale University Press, 1980.

Attempts to provide systematic philosophical foundations for the liberal state. Rejecting social contract theory and utilitarianism, he relies on the notion of a dialogue between persons making competing claims on scarce resources. Emphasis is on distributive justice, but also discusses genetic engineering, abortion, population control, and affirmative action. <DE/ED>

2   AIKEN, HENRY D., ed. Philosophy and Educational Development. Boston: Houghton Mifflin, 1966.

Anthology of articles by W. Kaufman, M. Scriven, A. Edel, P.A. Bertocci, K. Benne, and the editor on the nature of educational development. Questions of what is socially and personally learned, especially moral and ethical attitudes, are particularly relevant. <RS/ED>

3   ANDERSEN, MARY A.K. "An Analysis of the Treatment of Ethics in Selected Textbooks." Ph.D. diss., University of Michigan, 1979.

Speech communication textbooks for the basic course often allude to ethical questions and thus to philosophy. The purpose of this dissertation was to evaluate the actual ethical treatments within the books and particularly the depth of their development. Five texts were categorized in the highest category. <RS/ED>

4   ARISTOTLE. *Nichomachean Ethics.* Cambridge: Harvard University Press, 1983.
    Enduring study that established ethics as a discipline and as a practical science not strictly distinct from political science. Moral virtue and the importance of habit are primary themes, supplemented by analysis of happiness and friendship. <CC/ED>

5   ____. *The Rhetoric and Poetics.* New York: Random House, 1984.
    Has been of utmost influence, both directly and indirectly, upon Western rhetoric. Primary *ethical* arguments in favor of rhetoric are that it is useful for enabling truth to prevail over falsity, for providing audiences with special knowledge, for facilitating both sides of an issue, and for developing the capacity for persuasive argument. <RS/ED>

6   BAIER, K. *The Moral Point of View: A Rational Basis of Ethics.* New York: Random House, 1967.
    Explains moralities as forms of practical reasoning and social control. Provides procedures for making ethical decisions that include examining reasons, abstracting rules of reason, and using those rules in a *prima facie* sense in making personal and social decisions. <DE>

7   BARNSLEY, JOHN H. *The Social Reality of Ethics: The Comparative Analysis of Moral Codes.* London: Routledge, 1972.
    Major analysis of the *sociology* of ethics. Topics include "Criteria of Morality," "Elements of a Moral Code," "Theory and Practice," "Ethical Relativism," and "Review of Research," includes an in-depth examination of methods of sociological research. <RS/ED>

8   BAUM, ROBERT. *Ethical Arguments for Analysis.* New York: Holt, Rinehart & Winston, 1973.
    A trained philosopher brings classical methods to bear on modern topics such as "Gun Control," "Abortion and Sterilization," "Murder or Mercy," and related socio-ethical problems. The text illustrates how modern issues may be carefully analyzed with specific philosophical language and disciplined logic. <ED>

9   BENJAMIN, MARTIN. "Can Moral Responsibility Be Collective and Nondistributive?" *Social Theory and Practice* 4 (Fall 1976):93-106.

    Argues that theories of *collective* morality must grow out of theories of *individual* morality: "attributions of *moral* responsibility for collective action must ultimately be analyzed in terms of individual moral responsibility." Traditional individual moral theory is insufficient, however. <RS/ED>

10   BOK, SISSELA. *Lying: Moral Choice in Public and Private Life.* New York: Pantheon, 1977.

    Examines the many types of situations in which deception becomes an issue. Provides a justificatory method by which a person can test potentially deceptive practices and argues for the need for general honesty. <DE>

11   ____. *Secrets: On the Ethics of Concealment and Revelation.* New York: Pantheon, 1972.

    Inspects the notion of secrecy as it pervades personal and public life. Explores when confidentiality should be maintained and when breached. The book includes an excellent chapter on the risks of investigative journalism. <DE/ED>

12   BONHOEFFER, DIETRICH. *Ethics: What Is Meant by Telling the Truth.* New York: Macmillan, 1965.

    A subtle argument that truth is always contextual and thus cannot be reduced to a matter of nominally objective, but isolated, facts. <CC/ED>

13   BOWIE, NORMAN. "Applied Philosophy--Its Meaning and Justification," *Journal of Applied Philosophy* 1, no.1 (1982):1-18.

14   ____. *Making Ethical Decisions.* New York: McGraw-Hill, 1985.

    Anthology includes an excellent selection of excerpts from classical ethical works and articles from current moral philosophers. The book provides an easy introduction to ethical theory. Introductions to each section help the novice understand the basic questions reflected in personal ethical dilemmas. <DE/ED>

15   BRANDT, RICHARD B. *Ethical Theory.* Englewood Cliffs, N.J.: Prentice Hall, 1959.

    Swarthmore professor of philosophy provides textbook overview of the nature and purpose of ethical theory. Chapters include

"Two Tests of Ethical Principles: Consistency and Generality," "Can Science Solve All Ethical Problems?" "The Use of Authority in Ethics," and "Ethical Systems in Different Cultures and Their Development." Discusses such topics as determinism, noncognitivism, and relativism. <RS/ED>

16   BREAKWELL, GLYNNIS M.   "Moralities and Conflicts."   In *Morality in the Making: Thought, Action and the Social Context.* Edited by Helen Weinreich-Haste and Don Locke.   Chichester, England: John Wiley & Sons, 1983, 231-44.

17   BUBER, MARTIN.   *Between Man and Man.*   New York: Macmillan, 1965.

18   ____. *I and Thou.* New York: Scribner's, 1958.
     Philosophical description of the ethics of encounter or meeting. "Genuine responsibility exists only where there is responding," says Buber, by which he means *answering* and which he describes elsewhere as "genuine dialog." Drawing upon Jewish religious sources, the author presents religious existentialism which brings conversation and interpersonal relationships to the force of communication ethics. <RS/ED>

19   CALLAHAN, DANIEL, and H. TRISTRAM ENGLEHARDT, J. *The Roots of Ethics, Science, Religion and Values.*   New York: Plenum Press, 1981.
     Important collection of essays by modern thinkers such as A. MacIntyre, H. Jonas, S. Hauerwas, and S. Toulmin. Authors address the philosophical foundations of ethics, the importance and relevance of religion for ethical viewpoints, science's role in man's nature as knower and valuer, and the extent to which moral psychology can account for the human being's shift into the role of scientist. <AU/RS/ED>

20   CAPLAN, ARTHUR, and DANIEL CALLAHAN. *Ethics in Hard Times.* New York: Plenum Press, 1981.
     Anthology of essays by J. Rachels, P. Singer, J. Lieberson, R.A. Goldwin, D. Callahan, and others cross-examining the legitimacy of ethics: Can ethics really provide practical answers?   Why should human beings be moral? Can there be true economic justice in "hard times"? Can the human being, in the onslaught of increasing pollution, nuclear threats, heightened stress, over-population, and by increased avarice and tension, be *ethical?* <RS/ED>

21 CHILDRESS, JAMES. *Moral Responsibilities in Conflicts.* Baton Rouge: Louisiana State University Press, 1982.

Examines the different reasons offered to override some duties or responsibilities and support others. He uses three instances of conflict--nonviolent confrontation, war, and conscientious objection -- to illustrate the various moral justifications claimed to legitimize certain viewpoints. <ED>

22 CLOR, HARRY M. *Obscenity and Public Morality: Censorship in a Liberal Society.* Chicago: University of Chicago Press, 1969.

The many tributaries of the large river of "obscenity" include standards, the First Amendment, values, censorship, morality, moderation, and libertarianism. Focuses upon the crucial questions "What is the public interest in moral norms and moral character?" and "How is that interest best served?" <RS/ED>

23 COX, HARVEY, ed. *The Situation Ethics Debate.* Philadelphia: Westminster Press, 1968.

24 DANIELS, NORMAN, ed. *Reading Rawls: Critical Studies of a Theory of Justice.* New York: Basic Books, 1975.

Multifaceted analysis of influential modern ethical theorist John Rawls and his theory of justice. Commentary on Rawls by such leading thinkers as Nagel, Dworkin, and Hare presents both an analysis of Rawls's ethical thought and a critical commentary on specific problems and issues in writing. <RS/ED>

25 DONALDSON, DWIGHT M. *Studies in Muslim Ethics.* London: S.P.C.K., 1953.

26 DYCK, ARTHUR. *On Human Care: An Introduction to Ethics.* Nashville: Abingdon Press, 1977.

Clear introduction to issues such as normativity, relativism, and utilitarianism. Applies ethical theory to real world controversies such as population control and euthanasia. <CC/ED>

27 EMLER, NICHOLAS. "Morality and Politics: The Ideological Dimension in the Theory of Moral Development" and "Moral Character." In *Morality in the Making*: Thoughts, Actions, and the Social Contest. Edited by Helen Weinreich-Haste and Don Locke. Chichester, England: John Wiley & Sons, 1983, 47-72, 187-212.

28 ENGELS, FRIEDRICH. "Morality as Class Interest." In *Ethics in Perspective: A Reader*, Edited by Karsten J. Struhland and Paula Rosenberg Struhl. New York: Random House, 1951, 146-51.

29 FEINBERG, J. *Rights, Justice, and the Bounds of Liberty*. Princeton: Princeton University Press, 1980.
    This collection of previously published essays and papers covers issues in social and legal philosophy, bioethics, rights theory, and the theory of justice. The author analyzes the nature and value of rights; the relationship of rights to freedoms, duties, and obligations; rights claims and the rights of animals; the right to be born and the right to die; and the relationships among liberty, paternalism, and various formulations of "harm." <DE>

30 FISHKIN, J. *The Limits of Obligation*. New Haven: Yale University Press.
    Contends that the basic structure of individual morality and responsibility is incompatible with general obligations to society. In situations where large numbers of people are involved we need to rethink what actions--from minimum altruism to heroic sacrifice--are appropriate. <DE>

31 FISK, M. *Ethics and Society: A Marxist Interpretation of Value*. New York: New York University Press, 1980.
    An ambitious attempt to develop a Marxist ethics with a neutral rather than technical vocabulary on which broad agreement can be based. Argues that priority must be given to fulfilling people's essential needs. Primarily interested in elaborating the grounds for a relativistic ethics in which self-interest is served. Its theoretical scope and completeness rival that of Rawls's theory of justice. <DE>

32 FLETCHER, JOSEPH F. *Situation Ethics*. Philadelphia: Westminster Press, 1966.
    Situationism seeks to free ethics from rigid absolutist codes and permit individuality and particularity of circumstance to govern decision making. Fletcher's situationism promotes the *agape* concept of love as the controlling factor for ethical choices: "love provides the answers, defines the ends, and justifies the means." <PR/RS/ED>

33 FOOT, PHILIPPA, ed. *Theories of Ethics*. Oxford: Oxford University Press, 1967.
    Collection of significant essays by leading modern philosophers. G.E. Moore, John Rawls, and R.M. Hare are among

those who discuss primarily two widely debated philosophical issues--
the nature of moral judgment and the part played by social utility in
determining right and wrong. <AU/RS/ED>

34   FOUCAULT, MICHEL. *Language Counter-Memory, Practice:
     Selected Essays and Interviews.* Edited by Donald F. Bouchard.
     Translated by Donald F. Bouchard and Sherry Simon. Ithaca, N.Y.:
     Cornell University Press, 1977.

35   FRANKENA, WILLIAM K. *Ethics.*   Englewood Cliffs, N.J.:
     Prentice-Hall, 1973.
          Summary of ethical theory, major concepts, and most
     influential thinkers in classical philosophical ethics, written for general
     readers. <CC/ED>

36   FRIED, CHARLES. *An Anatomy of Values: Problems of Personal
     and Social Choice.* Cambridge: Harvard University Press, 1970.
          Such basic values as privacy, friendship, trust, art, and survival
     are examined within the philosophical context of evaluating means and
     ends, morality, and law. <RS/ED>

37   ____. *Right and Wrong.* Cambridge: Harvard University Press,
     1981.
          Division of the text into three sections--"Rights," "Wrongs," and
     "Roles"--permits analysis of types of perceived wrongs (the role of
     intention, the notion of harm, and the impact of lying) and the
     taxonomy of rights (evaluating wants, needs, virtue, compensation, and
     so on) and thus a penetrating analysis of assumed notions of positive
     and negative behavior. <RS/ED>

38   GERT, BERNARD. *The Moral Rules: A New Rational Foundation
     for Morality.* Rev. ed. New York: Harper, 1987.
          A systematic argument for a universal code of conduct that
     would be adopted by all rational human beings. Analysis of the role of
     reason, the virtue and vice dichotomy, moral rules and judgments, and
     the concepts of good and evil. A key chapter addresses the question
     "Why should one be moral?" <CC/ED>

39   GILLIGAN, CAROL. "New Maps of Development: New Vision of
     Maturity." *American Journal of Orthopsychiatry* 52, no. 2 (1982):199-
     212.
          Posits different priorities and assumptions in moral reasoning
     as practiced by boys and girls. Early male values may focus upon

justice and rights, whereas female values may more greatly emphasize care and response. In development psychology and in the examination of ethical theory these different mappings are significant pointers toward social understanding. <RS/ED>

40 GOODPASTER, K.E., and SAYRE, K.M. *Ethics and Problems of the 21st Century.* Notre Dame: University of Notre Dame Press, 1979.

These original essays address the problems associated with applying ethical theory to social and environmental issues. <CC>

41 HABERMAS, JURGEN. *Communication and the Evolution of Society.* Translated by Thomas McCarthy. Boston: Beacon Press, 1979.

42 HAUERWAS, STANLEY. *A Community of Character.* Notre Dame: University of Notre Dame Press, 1981.

Hauerwas is an important theological ethicist who continues to emphasize in this volume his concern for bringing virtue back into moral theory. The communities in which character is formed are crucial to him, and he pays particular attention to the role stories play in the development of virtuous behavior. <CC/ED>

43 JONAS, H. *The Imperative of Responsibility: In Search of an Ethics for the Technological Age.* Chicago: University of Chicago Press, 1984.

Highly debated thesis on global ethics in Germany. Argues that technological developments (nuclear weapons and international information) demand a new ethics that takes seriously our imminent destruction and global interdependence. Author anchors responsibility in a purposive nature that we are morally bound to preserve. A compelling argument that must be confronted by those in the media who make freedom the paramount good. <DE/ED>

44 JONES, WILLIAM T., FREDERICK SONTAG, MORTON BECKNER, and ROBERT J. FOGELIN, eds. *Approaches to Ethics: Representative Selections from Classical Times to the Present.* 2nd ed., New York: McGraw-Hill, 1969.

45 KANT, IMMANUEL. *Fundamental Principles of the Metaphysics of Morals.* New York: Bobbs-Merrill, 1949.

The influential eighteenth-century German philosopher argues that ethics is partly empirical and partly *a priori*. This work deals only with the *a priori* part as it is based entirely on the use of reason without recourse to experience. <RS/ED>

46 _____. *Groundwork of the Metaphysics of Morals.* New York: Harper & Row, 1964.

The German philosopher attempts to establish "the supreme principle of morality." Kant seeks in this text not to provide a complete metaphysics of morals but to lay out the foundation for the *a priori* portion of ethics which he carefully separates (see entry 45) from the empirical component of ethics. <RD/ED>

47 KAPLAN, ABRAHAM. *American Ethics and Public Policy.* New York: Oxford University Press, 1963.

Considers "bedrock" values and undergirding moral systems that provide the foundation for the national structure and policies of America. Values include vulgar pragmatism, moral absolutism, moralization, and so on. <RS/ED>

48 KOHLBERG, LAWRENCE. *The Philosophy of Moral Development: Essays in Moral Development.* New York: Harper & Row, 1983.

49 KUPPERMAN, J. *The Foundations of Morality.* London: George Allen & Unwin, 1983.

This is a compelling rationale for ethical theorizing. Although commonsense morality is not based on a clearly articulated theoretical foundation, morality cannot be critiqued or improved without redesigning the foundations. The book is primarily an attempt to explain the nature of ethical knowledge and articulate the ways in which ethical claims can be challenged and justified. <CC/DE/ED>

50 LODGE, RUPERT C. *Plato's Theory of Ethics.* New York: Shoestring Publishers, 1964.

Considers basic tenets of Platonist ethics: the highest good, moral standards, validity of moral judgement, value of the mind, value of the divine, preservation of the whole, and immortality, among others. Although somewhat dated, this book is considered a cornerstone text in the interpretation of Plato's ethical theory. <RS/ED>

51 LONG, EDWARD LEROY, Jr. *A Survey of Recent Christian Ethics.* Rev. ed. New York: Oxford University Press, 1982.

Update of the original 1967 volume which views normativity and relativism as central issues. Describes recent work about institutions, virtue, conscience, moral development, professional ethics, comparative religions, and liberation theology. Like the original edition, it is often rated the best introduction to Christian ethics. <CC/ED>

52   LYONS, D., ed. *Rights.* Belmont, Calif.: Wadsworth, 1979.
       This anthology contains essays by current philosophers on the nature of rights. The essays examine the nature of rights, claims for natural and self-evident rights, rights and justice, and the enforcement of rights. <DE>

53   MACINTYRE, ALISTAIR. *After Virtue: A Study in Moral Theory.* Notre Dame: University of Notre Dame Press, 1981.
       The best-selling volume in philosophy in recent years. MacIntyre's thesis is that Enlightenment individualism continues to dominate modern Western culture, and individual autonomy precludes the development of substantive ethics. Exceptional scholarship on Aristotle. Persuasive regarding Marx. <DE/ED>

54   _____. *A Short History of Ethics.* New York: Macmillan, 1964.
       Wide-ranging but readable summary of the history of ethics in the West from the Homeric Age to twentieth-century discussion. Separate chapters on major thinkers such as Plato, Aristotle, Kant, Mill, Hegel, Marx, Kierkegaard, and Nietzsche. <CC/ED>.

55   MACKIE, J.L. *Ethics: Inventing Right and Wrong.* New York: Penguin Books, 1977.

56   MAPPES, THOMAS A., and JANE S. ZEMBATY. *Social Ethics: Morality and Social Policy.* New York: McGraw-Hill, 1977.
       Significant collection of modern social issues such as abortion, euthanasia, the death penalty, mental illness, world hunger, and many others as considered by scholars, civic spokespersons, and Supreme Court justices. <RS/ED>

57   MILL, JOHN STUART. *On Liberty.* Chicago: Regnery, 1955.
       Perhaps the most influential essay on the question of the nature and limits of the power that can legitimately be exercised by society over the individual. <RS/ED>

58   _____. *Utilitarianism.* New York: Bobbs-Merrill, 1957.
       The famous nineteenth-century English philosopher maintained that acts that produce the greatest happiness for the

greatest number of persons are right and good. Argues that an act derives its moral worth not from its form but from its utility. Cornerstone theory for much of twentieth-century social ethics, which often elevates expediency above other values. <RS/ED>

59 MILLS, C. WRIGHT. *The Sociological Imagination.* London: Oxford University Press, 1967.
      Important work rejecting grand theory and abstracted empiricism. Instead the author advocates substantive social analyses that unearth genuine issues that are concretely historical and biographical. <CC/ED>

60 MOLTMAN, JURGEN. *On Human Dignity: Political Theology and Ethics.* Translated by H. Douglas Meeks. Philadelphia: Fortress Press, 1984.
      A major contemporary theologian who has been a foremost proponent of human rights. Important attempt to wrest human rights from its highly politicized context and establish it instead in a notion of human dignity. Emphasis on basic human needs, freedom, and community. He is particularly concerned about the relationship of freedom and power and includes an important chapter on meaningful work. <CC/ED>

61 NIEBUHR, REINHOLD. *Man's Nature and His Communities: Essays on the Dynamics of Man's Personal and Social Existence.* New York: C. Scribner's & Sons, 1965.
      Attempt by the noted theologian to account for human actions during the 1930's depression, two world wars, and the nuclear age. The application of theology to relevant political and social realities brought Niebuhr to this evaluation of human nature and a lay anthropological inspection of human direction, raison d'etre, and both ethical and unethical behavior. Because man is both a child of nature and a spirit who stands outside nature, he has the simultaneous capacity for selfless transcendence and self-preoccupied sin. <RS/ED>

62 NOZICK, ROBERT. *Anarchy, State, and Utopia.* New York: Basic Books, 1974.
      Presents a powerful defense of the "minimal state," arguing that the violations of individual rights brought about by the interference of the state can rarely be justified. He proposes a new theory of distributive justice and an integration of ethics, legal philosophy, and economic theory into a unified political philosophy. <DE>

63   OLSHEWSKY, T. *Foundations of Moral Decisions: A Dialogue.* Belmont, Calif.: Wadsworth, 1985.

This little book introduces the novice to ethical inquiry through an annotated dialogue format. Although the issues are within the realm of medical ethics and the dialogue participants are a physician, a lawyer, and a chaplain, the fundamental ethical theories raised are applicable to other situations. The annotations and study questions provide excellent introductory access to classical philosophy. The dialogue illustrates how the classical principles are reflected in discussion of practical issues. <DE>

64   OLSON, ROBERT G. *Ethics: A Short Introduction.* New York: Random House, 1978.

65   OUDEN, BERNARD DEN. *A Symposium on Ethics: The Role of Moral Values in Contemporary Thought.* Washington, D.C.: University Press of America, 1982.

Based on the Symposium, "The Role of Moral Values in Contemporary Thought" held at the University of Hartford on 28 April 1981, the volume consists of four essays each followed by comments by critics/respondents. The essays are "Values and Community" by M.W. Barnes; "Ethics in Journalism" by T.L. Glasser; "Life and Art" by J.B. Baker; and "War and Morality" by P.K. Breit. <UP/ED>

66   OUTKA, GENE. *Agape: An Ethical Analysis.* New Haven: Yale University Press, 1972.

Multifaceted inspection of notion of *agape*, one type of love as distinguished with classical Greek civilization and adopted by Christianity as a self-transcending divine love. Outka investigates Karl Barth's thought about agape and relates the concept to rules, self-love, justice, and other components as well as values within ethical systems. <RS/ED>

67   PLATO. *Gorgias.* Translated by Terence Irwin. Cambridge, Eng.: Oxford University Press, 1979.

Although seemingly more focused upon rhetoric than ethics, Plato's *Gorgias* outlines several key notions of the responsibilities and duties of the communicator. The orator must be knowledgeable about his subject. If justice is his subject, he not only must have knowledge about justice but must be intolerant of injustice. For Socrates the value of rhetoric is to make men aware of both the presence of and the cure for injustice. Hence rhetoric becomes a pedagogy of ethical behavior. <RS/ED>

68 ____. *The Republic of Plato*. Translated by Francis Macdonald Cornford. Oxford: Clarendon Press, 1965.

Perhaps the most significant treatise on political philosophy, *The Republic* embodies Plato's vision of an ideal society. Socrates claims that the just man, provided he has knowledge, may rule both himself and others and that his concern is not for himself alone. Notions of the just man and the just ruler are elaborated such that a theory of social ethics is espoused according to the training and actions of the individual, the relationships between individuals, and the collective action of classes in cooperation with philosopher guardians of the state. <RS/ED>

69 RAWLS, JOHN. *A Theory of Justice*. Cambridge: Harvard University Press, 1971.

The major twentieth-century theory of justice, offering an alternative to the utilitarian conception. The principles of justice Rawls sets forth are those that he claims the reasonable person would choose, were he cloaked in a "veil of ignorance," unaware of his own social status and natural assets and liabilities. <DE>

70 REIMAN, JEFFREY H. "Privacy, Intimacy, and Personhood." In *Today's Moral Problems*. 2d ed. Edited by Richard A. Wassertram. New York: Macmilan, 1979, 377-90.

71 ROBERTS, J.M. *A Short History of Morals*. London: Watts, 1920

72 RUSSELL, BERTRAND. *Human Society in Ethics and Politics*. New York: New American Library, 1955.

73 SIDGWICK, JOHN A. *Outlines of the History of Ethics*. Norwood, Pa.: Telegraph Books, 1985.

Distinguished Cambridge philosopher traces classical ethics from Greek and Greco-Roman beginnings through early Christian and medieval ethics to modern, primarily British ethicists and those European philosophers who have most influenced them. <RS/ED>

74 SIMMONS, JOHN A. *Moral Principles and Political Obligations*. Princeton: Princeton University Press, 1979.

Reviews major theories in political moral philosophy, from Locke through Nozick, examining the problem of political obligation. Finds that principles of consent, fair play, gratitude, and the duty of justice cannot justify claims that most citizens have obligations or duties to support and comply with our political institutions. <DE/ED>

75 SWOMLEY, JOHN H. *Liberation Ethics*. New York: Macmillan, 1972.
    Evaluation of the political ethics and relationships between oppressor and oppressed. Examples, whether from Marx and revolutionary thinkers or the nonviolent civil disobedience movements of Gandhi and King, emphasize the notion of changing power relationships, freedom from enmity, and the value of both personal and social transformation. <RS/ED>

76 TAYLOR, P.W. *Principles of Ethics: An Introduction*. Encino, Calif.: Dickenson, 1975.
    Well-written chapters for beginners. Provides helpful definitions of ethics, morals, and values. Good overview of utilitarianism and Kantian ethics. <DE>

77 THIROUX, JACQUES P. *Ethics, Theory and Practice*. New York: Macmillan, 1980.

78 WILLIAMS, BERNARD. *Morality: An Introduction to Ethics*. New York: Harper & Row, 1972.

79 WILLIAMS, G.L., ed. *John Stuart Mill on Politics and Society*. New York: International Publications Service, 1976.

I B. PROFESSIONAL ETHICS: BUSINESS, LEGAL, MEDICAL, GOVERNMENTAL, SCIENTIFIC, AND ENGINEERING

80 ABRAMS, NATALIE, and MICHAEL D. BUCKNER, eds.
Medical Ethics: A Clinical Textbook and Reference for the Health
Care Professions. Cambridge: MIT Press, 1983.

81 BAYLES, MICHAEL. Professional Ethics. Belmont Calif.:
Wadsworth, 1981.
    Overview of general ethical issues of concern to professionals:
duties to clients and the public, relationships between professional
norms and ordinary ethical principles, obligations for maintaining a
profession's vitality, regulation, the notion of service, and disciplining
unprofessional behavior. <CC/DE/ED>

82 BEAUCHAMP, TOM L. Ethics and Public Policy. Englewood
Cliffs, N.J.: Prentice-Hall, 1975.

83 BENSON, GEORGE C. Business Ethics in America. Lexington,
Mass.: Lexington Books, 1982.

84 BOK, SISSELA. "Whistleblowing and Professional Responsibilities." In *Ethics Teaching in Higher Education*. Edited by Daniel Callahan and Sissela Bok. New York: Plenum Press 1980, 277-98.

85 BOWIE, NORMAN. *Business Ethics*. Englewood Cliffs, N.J.: Prentice-Hall, 1982.

86 BUXTON, EDWARD. *Creative Ethics*. New York: Executive Communications, 1975.

87 THE CENTER FOR BUSINESS ETHICS AT BENTLEY COLLEGE. Power and Responsibility in the American Business System: Highlights of Second National Conference on Business Ethics." In *Business Ethics Report*. Waltham, Mass.: Bentley College, 1978.

88 CHALK, ROSEMARY, MARK S. FRANKEL, and SALLY B. CHAFER. *AAAS Professional Ethics Project: Professional Activities in Scientific and Engineering Societies*. Washington, D.C.: American Association for the Advancement of Science, 1980.

89 CLAPP, JANE. *Professional Ethics and Insignia*. Metuchen, N.J.: Scarecrow Press, 1974.

90 CULVER, CHARLES M., and BERNARD GERT. *Philosophy in Medicine: Conceptual and Ethical Issues in Medicine and Psychology*. New York: Oxford University Press, 1982.
    Important collaboration between a major moral theorist and a leading psychologist, both of whom are administrators of the Dartmouth Ethics Institute. Most philosophical volume of the leading medical ethics texts. <ED>

91 DEGEORGE, RICHARD T. *Business Ethics*. 2d ed. New York: Macmillan, 1986.

92 DIENER, E., and R. CRANDALL. *Ethics in Social and Behavioral Research*. Chicago: University of Chicago Press, 1978.
    How may educated and concerned researchers adopt the best safeguards against scientific abuses? Issues investigated include harm to participants, informed consent, privacy, deception of participants, honesty, accuracy, reliability of sample, and the overall relationship between science and society. <UN/ED>

93   DRUCKER, PETER. "Ethical Chic." *Forbes*. 14 September 1981, 160-73.

94   EUBEN, PETER. Philosophy and the Professions." *Democracy*, April 1981, 112-27.

95   FLORES, ALBERT, and DEBORAH C. JOHNSON. "Collective Responsibility and Professional Roles." *Ethics* 93 (April 1983) :537-45.

96   FREUDBERG, DAVID. "Ministering to the Corporation." *Across the Board* 21, no. 11(1984):14-19.

97   GARRETT, THOMAS M., and RICHARD J. KLONOSKI. *Business Ethics*. 2d ed. Englewood Cliffs, N.J.: Prentice-Hall, 1986.

98   GOLDMAN, ALAN H. *The Moral Foundations of Professional Ethics*. Totowa, N.J.: Rowman & Littlefield, 1980.
        Are professional ethics unique?   Although professionals themselves often tend toward differentiation, Goldman argues for continuity among the professions.   The names and principles of professional ethics arise from moral theory. Separate chapters cover medical, legal, business, and government ethics. <CC/DE/ED>

99   GOTHIE, DANIEL L. "A Selected Bibliography of Applied Ethics in the Professions, 1950-1970." Charlottesville: University Press of Virginia, 1973.

100 HOFFMAN, W. MICHAEL, and JENNIFER M. MOORE. *Business Ethics: Readings in Corporate Morality*.   New York: McGraw-Hill, 1984.

101 HUNT, SHELBY D., and LAWRENCE B. CHONKO. "Marketing and Machiavellianism." *Journal of Marketing* 48, no. 3 (1984):30-42.

102 JOHNSEN, ALBERT P. *Responsibilities of Medical Practice*. San Francisco: University of California Press, 1984.

103 KELLY, MICHAEL J.   *Legal Ethics and Legal Education*. Hastings-on-Hudson, N.Y.: Hastings Center, 1980.

104 LEBACQZ, KAREN. *Professional Ethics: Power and Paradox*. Nashville: Abingdon Press, 1985.

105 LERNER, MAX. "The Shame of the Professions." *Saturday Review*, 5 November 1975, 10-29.

106 MC CONNELL, TERRANCE C. *Moral Issues in Health Care: An Introduction to Medical Ethics*. Belmont, Calif.: Wadsworth, 1982.

107 MC KEE, CARRIE. "New Philosophers Apply Ethics to Professions." *Humanities Report*, July 1981, 12-15.

108 MAWHINNEY, T.C. "Philosophical and Ethical Aspects of Organizational Behavior Management: Some Evaluative Feedback." *Journal of Organizational Behavior Management* 6, no. 1 (1984):5-31.

109 MAY, WILLIAM F. "Code, Covenant, Contract, or Philanthropy." *Hastings Center Report* 5 (December 1975):29-38.

110 MEYER, PHILIP. "Corporate Espionage: When Market Research Goes Too Far." *Business Marketing* 69, no. 10 (1984):50-66.

111 MILLER, WILLIAM H. "Business' New Link: Ethics and the Bottom Line." *Industry Week* 40 no. 9 (1984)49-53.

112 NADER, RALPH, and KENNETH R. ANDREWS. "Reforming Corporate Governance: Difficulties in Overseeing Ethical Policy." *California Management Review* 26, no. 4 (1984):111-25.

113 NORRIS, JOSEPH C., Jr. "The Ethical Struggle: Business Conduct, Public Responsibility, and Regulation." *Life Association News* 79, no. 5 (1984):18.

114 NORTH, AMANDA, ed. "The Ethics Controversy." *Business Today* 14, no. 1 (1977).
Special Issue: Business Ethics.

115 OPINION RESEARCH CORPORATION. *Implementation and Enforcement of Codes of Ethics in Corporations and Associations*. Princeton: Opinion Research Corp., 1980.

116 THE PUBLIC INTEREST. "Ethics in Business, Education, and Politics." *The Public Interest* 63 (Spring 1981).
Special Issue: Ethics in the Professions.

117 RAINEY, HAL. "Reward Preferences among Public and Private Managers: In Search of the Service Ethic." *American Review of Public Administration* 16, no. 4 (1982):288-302.

118 SANDERSON, GLEN R., and IRIS I. VARNER. "What's Wrong with Corporate Codes of Conduct?" *Management Accounting* 66, no. 1 (1984):28-35.

119 SCHILIT, HOWARD M. "Deviant Behavior and Misconduct of Professionals." *Woman CPA* 46, no. 2 (1984):20-24.

120 SCHORNHORST, F.T. "The Lawyer and the Terrorist: Another Ethical Dilemma." *Indiana Law Journal* 53 (Summer 1978).
Special issue: Legal aspects of media and terrorism.

121 SHERWIN, DOUGLAS. "The Ethical Roots of the Business System." *Harvard Business Review*, November-December 1983, 183-93.

122 SNOEYENBOS, MILTON, ROBERT ALMEDER, and JAMES HUMBER, eds. *Business Ethics: Corporate Values and Society.* Buffalo, N.Y.: Prometheus Books, 1983.

123 SOLOMAN, ROBERT C., and KRISTINE R. HANSON. *Above the Bottom Line: An Introduction to Business Ethics.* New York: Harcourt Brace Jovanovich, 1983.

124 THOMAS, MICHAEL. "Know Where You Stand on Ethics." *Purchasing World* 28, no. 10 (1984):90-91.

125 TIME. "Whatever Happened to Ethics?" *Time,* 25 May 1987, 16-41.
Special issue focuses on what is wrong with American professional ethics in business (for example, Wall Street financier Ivan Boesky), religion (Jim and Tammy Bakker), politics ("Irangate" cover up, Gary Hart controversy), military (U.S. Marine security violations at U.S. embassy in Moscow), and engineering (*Challenger* disaster).

126 VEATCH, ROBERT M. *Case Studies in Medical Ethics.* Cambridge: Harvard University Press, 1977.

127 _____. *A Theory of Medical Ethics.* New York: Basic Books, 1982.

128 WAKIN, MALHAM M., ed. *War, Morality and the Military Profession.* Boulder, Colo.: Westview Press, 1981.

129   WILLBERN, YORK. "Types and Levels of Public Morality." *Public Administration Review* 44 (March-April 1984):102-8.

I C. COMMUNICATION AND MASS MEDIA ETHICS: CODES, ADVERTISING, PUBLIC RELATIONS, FILM, PRINT, PUBLISHING, AND RADIO

130 AGEE, WARREN K., PHILLIP H. AULT, and EDWIN EMERY. *Maincurrents in Mass Communications*. New York: Harper & Row, 1986.

131 ALTHEIDE, DAVID L. *Media Power*. Newbury Park, Calif.: Sage, 1985.
    Explains how both culture and consciousness take on a mediated existence central to society. Chapters include "The TV News Code and the Information Order" and "The Media as a Social Force." <ED>

132 AMERICAN LEGAL FOUNDATION. *Terrorism and the Media*. Washington, D.C.: American Legal Foundation, 1985.

133 ARTERTON, CHRISTOPHER F. *Teledemocracy*. Newbury Park, Calif.: Sage, 1987.
    A comprehensive review and critical appraisal of proposed technological solutions to political problems, including the ethical and

social tensions they create. Chapters include "The Debate over Technology and Democracy" and "Teaching Citizenship through Technology." <GG/ED>

134 ASUNCTION-LANDE, NOBLEZA C. *Ethical Perspectives and Critical Issues in Intercultural Communication.* Annandale, Va.: Speech Communication Association, 1980.

135 AYER, ALFRED. "Effects of the Mass Media on Individual Morality." *Educational Broadcasting International* 7, no. 4 (1974):188-93.
    An analysis of how media influence moral development and individual character formation. <HB/ED>

136 BAGDIKIAN, BEN H. *The Media Monopoly.* Boston: Beacon Press, 1983.
    The first half of the book documents extensively the scope of control of the mass media by the fifty largest corporations. The second explores the implications of monopoly for society, the media, and the messages of communication institutions. Advertising subsidized media are particularly scrutinized. <UN/ED>

137 BAKER, ROBERT K., and SANDRA J. BALL. *Mass Media Hearings: A Report to the National Commission on the Causes and Prevention of Violence.* Washington, D.C.: U.S. Government Printing Office, 1969.

138 BAKER, SAM S. *The Permissible Lie: The Inside Truth about Advertising.* Boston: Beacon Press, 1971.

139 BAUDE, P., ed. "Terrorism and the Media." *Indiana Law Journal* 53 (Summer 1978).
    Special issue: Legal aspects of media coverage of terrorism. <ED>

140 BEAUCHAMP, THOMAS. "Manipulative Advertising." *Business and Professional Ethics Journal* 3, nos. 3-4 (1984).

141 BECKER, BORIS W., and PATRICK E. CONNOR. "Personal Values of the Heavy User of Mass Media." *Journal of Advertising Research* 21, no. 5 (9181):37-43.
    Results of a value survey administered to fifty-eight subjects demonstrate that personal values influence the subjects' media-usage

behavior. Data collected on the time spent by subjects watching television and reading magazines were compared with their personal values. <UN/ED>

142 BERMAN, RONALD. *Advertising and Social Change*. Newbury Park, Calif.: Sage, 1981.

The author claims that advertising has replaced traditional institutions--home, church, and state--as a guide to what we are and what we expect to be. Scrutinizes federal regulatory attempts, theories of social control, and guidelines for evaluating advertising. <AU/ED>

143 BERTRAND, JEAN CLAUDE. "Ethics in International Communications." *Intermedia* 13, no. 2 (1985):9-14.

144 _____. "Media Ethics in Perspective." *Journal of Mass Media Ethics* 2, no. 1 (1986-87):7-16.

145 BIERSTEDT, ROBERT. "The Ethics of Cognitive Communication." *Journal of Communication* 13, no. 3 (9163):199-203.

146 BLACK, JAY, and RALPH BARNEY. "The Case against Mass Media Codes of Ethics." *Journal of Mass Media Ethics* 1, no. 1 (1985-86):27-36.

Insights from the First Amendment and developmental psychology are utilized to argue that, whatever value codes of ethics hold for mass media, they present serious difficulties by inculcating substantial ethical values in individual journalists and in the profession as a whole. <UN/ED>

147 BLUM, ELEANOR, and CLIFFORD G. CHRISTIANS. "Ethical Problems in Book Publishing." *Library Quarterly* 51, no. 2 (1982):155-69.

Inductive inquiry into the practices of 140 people working in book publishing. Four explicit concerns emerged: (1) promoting materials truthfully, (2) morally resolving tensions between editors and authors, (3) treating support personnel fairly, and (4) instilling quality in all editorial and production processes. <CC/ED>

148 BLUNDEN, MARGARET. "Technology and Values: Problems and Options." *Futures* (U.K.) 16, no. 4 (1984):418-24.

149 BOORSTIN, DANIEL J. *The Image: Or What Happened to the American Dream?* New York: Atheneum, 1962.

150 BOSMAJIAN, HAIG, ed. *The Principles and Practice of Freedom of Speech.* 2d ed. New York: University Press of America, 1983.

151 BOVENTER, HERMANN. "New Media, the Morality of Freedom and Political Education." *Communication* 9, no 2 (1986):247-70.

152 No entry

153 BROWN, CHARLENE J., TREVOR R. BROWN, and WILLIAM L. RIVERS. *The Media and the People.* New York: Holt, Rinehart & Winston, 1978.
    Lengthy inspection of the social responsibility of the press augments discussions on media and social control, sex and violence on television, and objectivity. Includes readable summary of the importance of the Hutchins Commission. <UN/ED>

154 CALLAHAN, D., W. GREEN, B. JENNINGS, and M. LINSKY. *Congress and the Media: The Ethical Connection.* New York: Hastings Center, 1985.

155 CARTER, T. BARTON, MARC C. FRANKLIN, and JAY B. WRIGHT. *The First Amendment and the Fourth Estate: The Law of Mass Media.* Mineola, N.Y.: Foundation Press, 1985.

156 CASEBIER, ALAN, and JANET CASEBIER, eds. *Social Responsibilities of the Mass Media.* Washington, D.C.: University Press of America, 1978.
    Selected papers from the Conference on Mass Media Responsibility held at the University of Southern California in the spring of 1976. Includes chapters on professional press ethics, accuracy and imbalance in 1976 election news coverage, images of women, ethnic group depiction, pro- and antisocial entertainment images, producers' responsibilities, and program evaluation standards. <CC/ED>

157 CHESBRO, JAMES W. "A Construct for Assessing Ethics in Communication." *Central States Speech Journal* 20, no. 2 (1969):104-15.

158 CHRISTIANS, CLIFFORD G. "Beyond Quandaries: A Plea for Normative Ethics." *Mass Comm Review* 6, no. 3 (1979):28-31.

Claims that examination of mass communication ethics must move beyond (1) description of situations and (2) quandaries. Formulation of normativity is required. <CC/ED>

159 _____. "Codes of Ethics and Accountability." In *Press Theory in the Liberal Tradition*. Urbana: University of Illinois Press, 1986, ch. 9.
Social history of professional media codes, especially those of the SDX/SPJ and National Association of Broadcasters. Three types of accountability are distinguished, and an argument is made in defense of codes that make peers accountable to one another. <CC/ED>

160 _____. "Enforcing Media Codes." *Journal of Mass Media Ethics* 1, no. 1 (1985-86):14-21.
The long-standing debates over how to enforce codes of ethics reflect a serious misunderstanding of the nature of accountability. Fuzziness about accountability has allowed the quantity of codes but not the quality or the application of code principals to expand. Greater precision in different forms and degrees of accountability to government, peers, and public is required. <CC/ED>

161 _____. "Fifty Years of Scholarship in Media Ethics." *Journal of Communication* 27, no. 4 (1977):19-29.
The study of media ethics began in the 1920s as a branch of study in schools and departments of journalism. During the 1930s objectivity became the keystone of journalistic morality. After World War II, relevance and thoroughness became the supreme standards. The key arguments of current debate and the author's own proposals conclude. <CC/ED>

162 _____. "On Penultimates and Golden Means in Media Ethics." *Social Responsibility: Journalism, Law, Medicine* (Washington and Lee University) 6 (1980):5-15.
Indicates how two ethical theorists, Aristotle and John Rawls, are not strictly academic, but can illuminate the moral issues faced daily by professional journalists. <CC/ED>

163 CHRISTIANS, CLIFFORD G., MARK FACKLER, and KIM ROTZOLL. *Media Ethics: Cases and Moral Reasoning*. 2d ed. New York: Longman, 1987.
Eighty-one case studies with commentaries cover the major issues in news, entertainment, public relations, and advertising. Introductory material acquaints students with the major strains of

Western ethical theory and the Potter box, an instrument for analyzing ethical situations and logically justifying conclusions. <CC/ED>

164 CHRISTIANS, CLIFFORD G., and KIM B. ROTZOLL. "Ethical Issues in the Film Industry." *In Current Research in Film.* Edited by Bruce Austin, Vol. 2. Norwood, N.J.: Ablex, 1985, 225-36.

Study of ethical decision making by 212 company executives in the film industry. Key problems include financing, production, and sales. Ellul's ethic of "efficiency" used in describing cinema industry. <CC/ED>

165 CHRISTIANS, CLIFFORD G., QUENTIN SCHULTZE, and NORMAN SIMS. "Community, Epistemology, and Mass Media Ethics." *Journalism History* 5, no. 2 (1979):38-41, 65-67.

The origins of our current interest in mass media ethics are embedded in the Progressive Era. Given those roots, the need to resolve debates over epistemology and community is present if ethics theory is to advance significantly.

166 CHRISTIANS, CLIFFORD G., and GUDMOND GJELSTEN. *Media Ethics and the Church.* Kristiansand, Norway: International Mass Media Institute Publications, 1981.

Proceedings of an international conference especially represented by third world countries. Theory, print media, broadcasting, advertising, performing arts, and the new international order all included within three areas--Christian perspectives, secular debates, and practical models. <CC/ED>

167 CLARK, DAVID G., and WILLIAM B. BLANKENBURG. *You & Media: Mass Communication and Society.* San Francisco: Canfield Press, 1973.

Of particular relevance are Chapter 6, "The New Ethics," and Chapter 7, "The Peculiarities of Freedom."

168 CLOTFELTER, J., and G.G. PETERS. "Mass Media and the Military: Selected Ratings of Fairness." *Journalism Quarterly* 51 (Summer 1974): 332-33.

169 COLLINS, RICHARD, JAMES CURRAN, NICHOLAS GARNHAM, PADDY SCANNELL, PHILIP SCHLESINGER, and COLIN SPARKS. *Media, Culture, and Society.* Newbury Park, Calif.: Sage, 1986.

A selective compilation of articles published between 1979 and 1985 in the journal of the same name. Authors include editors of the volume (listed above) and Stuart Hall, John Corner, Michelle Mattelart, Raymond Williams and others. Relevant chapters include "'Terrorism' and the State: A Case Study of the Discourses of Television" and "The Impact of Advertising on the British Mass Media." <PR/ED>

170 *Communication* 6 (1981).
Special issue: Media ethics in the United States and abroad. <DE>

171 COOK, ZENA, et al. *Impact of Advertising: Implications for Consumer Education.* Washington, D.C.: Public Interest Economics Center, 1978. [ERIC: ED162165]
Review and analysis of advertising's effects upon consumer choice, national values, and life-styles. Intended to aid consumer educators and related professionals. Includes implications of corporate-sponsored and television advertising upon politics and social affairs. <CSS/ED>

172 CORRY, JOHN. "Can the People Trust the Media?" *New York Times,* 6 June, 1985; Sect. 3, p. 25.

173 CULLEN, MAURICE R., Jr. *Mass Media and the First Amendment.* Debuque, Iowa: Wm. C. Brown, 1981.

174 CURRAN, CHARLES. *A Seamless Robe: Broadcasting Philosophy and Practice.* London: Collins, 1979.

175 DEETZ, STANLEY. "Keeping the Conversation Going: The Principle of Dialectic Ethics." *Communications* 7, no. 2 (1983): 263-88.
A principle that simultaneously provides ethics *of* communication and *for* communication is posited. Recent writings in hermeneutics and critical theory are reviewed for relevant discussion, debate, and implication. <UN/ED>

176 DELATTRE, EDWIN J. "Ethics in the Information Age." *Public Relations Journal* 40, no. 6 (1984): 12-15.

177   DENNIS, EVERETT E. "Politics of Media Credibility." Speech delivered at the Journalism Ethics Institute, Washington and Lee University, March 1986.
      Manuscript available from Gannett Center for Media Studies, Columbia University, 2950 Broadway, New York, NY 10027.

178   DENNIS, EVERETT E., ARNOLD H. ISMACH, and DONALD M. GILLMOR, eds. *Enduring Issues in Mass Communication*. St. Paul, Minn.: West Publishing, 1978.
      Anthology of thirty-five essays and studies grouped into sections on the media's impact on society, media roles and performances, and media reforms and innovations. <UN/ED>

179   DENNIS, EVERETT, E., and J.C. MERRILL. *Basic Issues in Mass Communication*. New York: Macmillan, 1983.

180   ELLIOTT-BOYLE, DENI.   "A Conceptual Analysis of Ethics Codes." *Journal of Mass Media Ethics* 1, no. 1 (1985-86): 22-26.
      Codes necessarily state standards of professional practice, but the term *standards* is ambiguous. "Standards of professional practice" can mean minimal expectations for all practitioners or, at the other extreme, the perceived ideal toward which practitioners should strive. Code production is healthy because practitioners are encouraged to make a critical analysis of their profession. <UN/ED>

181   ELLIS, GODFREY J., "Youth in the Electronic Environment: An Introduction." *Youth and Society* 15, no. 1 (1983): 3-12.
      Discusses the notion of an "electronic environment" surrounding contemporary adolescents. How are the stereo, television, radio, and video games influencing adolescent development and growth? <CMG/ED>

182   ELLUL, JACQUES.   *Propaganda: The Formation of Men's Attitudes*. East Hanover, N.J.: Vintage Books, 1965.
      A significant attempt to broaden the definition of propaganda beyond the examples of Goebbels, modern advertising, and mainstream concepts to include *covert* propaganda, such as news and common entertainment, which are often not recognized as manipulative and prejudiced. <CC/ED>

183   EMERY, MICHAEL, and TED CURTIS SMYTHE. *Readings in Mass Media: Concepts and Issues in the Mass Media*. 6th ed. Dubuque, Iowa: Wm. C. Brown, 1986.

184 ESHELMAN, DAVID. "Freedom of Speech Bibliography: July 1977-June 1978; Articles, Books, Newsletters, Court Cases, and Dissertations." In *Free Speech Yearbook, 1978*, Edited by Greg Phifer. Annandale, VA. Speech Communication Association, 1978, 125-52.

185 EVANS, LAURENCE. *The Communication Gap: The Ethics and Machinery of Public Relations and Information.* London: Charles Knight, 1973.

186 FORTNER, ROBERT S. "Physics and Metaphysics in an Information Age: Privacy, Dignity and Identity." *Communication* 9, no. 2 (1986):173-94.

187 FRYE, NORTHROP. "The Renaissance of Books." *Visible Language* 7, no. 3 (1974): 225-40.
      Although the central theme is how the paperback revolution has broadened the role of books in society, the social effects of television and radio, and the concomitant questions raised, are contrasted. <HOD/ED>

188 GERBNER, GEORGE, and MARSHA SIEFERT. *World Communications: A Handbook.* New York: Longman, 1984.
      Part 1 describes communication and information policies of various world constituencies. Part 2 contains papers on the international flow of news and images. Part 3 encompasses effects of telecommunications technologies upon national policies and international relations. Part 4 focuses on the role of communications systems in national development. <RR/ED>

189 GORDON, GEORGE N. *Erotic Communications: Studies in Sex, Sin and Censorship.* New York: Hastings House, 1980.
      Examines facets of communication about human sexual behavior. History, contemporary mass media portrayals, and the legal rubric of regulation and censorship are all examined. <RR/ED>

190 GREER, HERB. "Terrorism and the Media." *Encounter,* August 1982, 67-74.

191 HAIMAN, FRANKLYN S. *Speech and Law in a Free Society.* Chicago: University of Chicago Press, 1981.

192 HANEY, ROBERT W. *Comstockery in America: Patterns of Control and Censorship.* New York: DeCapo, 1974

193 HARRISON, JOHN M. "Media, Men, and Morality." *Review of Politics* 36, no. 2 (1974): 250-55.

194 HASELDEN, KYLE. *Morality and the Mass Media.* Nashville: Broadman, 1972.
     Censorship, obscenity, commercialism, and the portrayal of sex and violence are special concerns. Advocates enlightened awareness of media, rather than aggressive protest, from a primarily Protestant perspective. <CC/ED>

195 HEIBERT, RAY ELDON, and CAROL REUSS, ed. *Impact of Mass Media.* White Plains, N.Y.: Longman, 1985.
     Anthology of sixty essays by a broad spectrum of authors organized into sixteen sections, one of which is "Mass Media and Ethics." Issues include press freedom versus press responsibility; sex and sensationalism; government control of media versus media control of government; media as wasteland culture; minorities and media; women and media; televangelism as amplified proselytizing. <PR/ED>

196 HORNIK, ROBERT C. "Mass Media Use and the 'Revolution of Rising Expectations': A Reconsideration of the Theory." *Communication Research* 4, no. 4 (1977): 387-414.
     A three-year study of El Salvadoran junior high school students is summarized. The relationship between their early mass media use and subsequent change in social expectations is analyzed. <MH/ED>

197 HOWARD, CAROLE, and WILMA MATHEWS. "Ethics: The Golden Rule of Media Relations." In *On Deadline: Managing Media Relations.* New York: Longman, 1985.

198 HOWELL, WILLIAM S. Foreword to *Ethical Perspectives and Critical Issues in Intercultural Communication* Edited by Nobleza C. Asuncion-Lande, Annandale, VA. Speech Communications Association, 1980.

199 HUXLEY, ALDOUS. *Brave New World.* New York: Bantam, 1939.

200 INTERNATIONAL PRESS INSTITUTE. Terrorism and the Media. London: International Press Institute, 1980.

201 JAKSA, JAMES, and MICHAEL W. PRITCHARD. "The Perspective of the Deceived: An Ethical Analysis." Paper presented at the meeting of the Speech Communication Association, Louisville, Kentucky, November 1982.

202 JAMIESON, KATHLEEN HALL, and KARLYN KOHRS CAMPBELL. The Interplay of Influence: Mass Media and Their Publics in News, Advertising, Politics. Belmont, Calif.: Wadsworth, 1983.

203 JOHANNESEN, RICHARD L. "Ethical Responsibility in Communication: A Selected Annotated Basic Bibliography" Annandale, VA. Speech Communicative Module, ERIC Clearinghouse on Reading and Communication Skills. [ED140376]

204 _____. Ethics and Persuasion: Selected Readings. Prospect Heights, Ill.: Waveland Press, 1981.

205 _____. Ethics in Human Communication. Prospect Heights, Ill.: Waveland Press, 1987.
Outlines four perspectives from which ethical judgments about communication can by made. Scope includes interpersonal to mass communication, with emphasis upon the former. Wide scope of research evident in useful footnotes and bibliography. <CC/ED>

206 _____. "Some Sources on Ethical and Moral Issues in Mass Communication." In Ethics, Morality and the Media: Reflections on American Culture. Edited by Lee Thayer. New York: Hastings House, 1980, 286-92.

207 Journal of Mass Media Ethics.
Journal founded in 1985 is published twice yearly. Available from Ralph Barney, Department of Communications, Brigham Young University, Provo, UT 84602.

208 KEY, WILSON BRYAN. The Clam-Plate Orgy: And Other Subliminals the Media Use to Manipulate Your Behavior. Englewood Cliffs, N.J.: Prentice-Hall, 1980.

209 _____. Media Sexploitation. Englewood Cliffs, N.J.: Prentice-Hall, 1976.

Attempts to demonstrate how some advertisers are surreptitiously using theories of human behavior to manipulate and direct consumer buying behavior. <UN/ED>

210 _____. Subliminal Seduction. Englewood Cliffs, N.J.: Prentice-Hall, 1972.

Purports to expose numerous instances in which advertising has used subliminal messages and imagery, primarily of a sexual nature, to sell products. Research includes numerous ads magnified to reveal possible hidden messages and symbols. <UN/ED>

211 KIVIKURU, ULLAMAIJA, and TAPIO VARIS, ed. Approaches to International Communication. Helsinki: Finnish National Commission for UNESCO, 1986.

Collection of important essays by twenty-one authors from almost as many countries. Subjects include journalism ethics, transborder data flow policy, international law and mass communication, dependency and cultural choice, and national information policy. <ED>

212 KNAPP, MARK L., and MARK E. COMEDENA. "Telling It Like It Isn't: A Review of Theory and Research on Deceptive Communications." Human Communication Research 5, no. 3 (1978):270-85.

213 KNOPF, TERRY A. "Media Myths on Violence." Columbia Journalism Review 9, no. 1 (1970):17-25.

214 KRUGER, ARTHUR N. "The Ethics of Persuasion: A Re-examination." Communication Education 16, no. 4 (1967):295-305.

215 LEVITT, THEODORE. "The Morality (?) of Advertising." Harvard Business Review 48 (July-August 1970):84-92.

216 LIPPMAN, WALTER. Public Opinion. New York: Harcourt, Brace, 1922.

Although published long before the advent of television, this classic is perhaps the best known and most influential treatise on the nature of collective attitudes as interactive with mass media, prior to World War II. <ED>

217   MC CLELLAN, MICHAEL. "Social Responsibility and the New Technology." *Mass Comm Review* 10, no. 3 (9183):13-22
An analysis of Reinhold Niebuhr's thought and his work on the Commission on Freedom of the Press. The role of new technology, an assessment of the present environment, and the relationship between the two are emphasized. <RR/ED>

218   MC CLINTICK, DAVID. *Indecent Exposure: A True Story of Hollywood and Wall Street.* New York: Dell, 1982.

219   MC DONALD, DONALD. "The Media's Conflict of Interests." *Center Magazine* 9 (1976):15-35.

220   MC KERNS, JOSEPH P. "Media Ethics: A Bibliographical Essay." *Journalism History* 5 (Summer 1978).
Special Issue.

221   MANDER, JERRY. *Four Arguments for the Elimination of Advertising.* Urbana: University of Illinois, Department of Advertising, 1979.

222   MARSHALL, CARTER L. *Toward an Educated Health Consumer: Mass Communication and Quality in Medical Care.*   Fogarty International Series on the Teaching of Preventive Medicine, vol. 7. Bethesda, Md.: Fogarty International Center. [ERIC: ED151510]

223   MARTIN, L.J., and A.G. CHAUDHARY. *Comparative Mass Media Systems.* New York: Longman, 1983.
Nineteen specialists compare the role and environment of mass media in three geographical systems (the West, Communist countries, the Third World) in terms of six key concepts: news, the role of mass media, educational and persuasive function media, entertainment, press freedom, and economics. <RR>

224   *MEDIA & VALUES.*
A quarterly review of media issues, trends, and ethical questions published in Los Angeles by the Center for Communications Ministry. The dimension of underlying social and religious values is emphasized. Available from Center of Communications Ministry, 1962 S. Shenandoah, Los Angeles, CA 90034. <RR/ED>

225   MERRILL, JOHN C., and RALPH L. LOWENSTEIN. *Media, Messages and Men.* New York: Longman, 1979.

226 MEYER, PHILIP. *Editors, Publishers, and Newspaper Ethics.* Washington, D.C.: American Society of Newspaper Editors, 1983.

227 MIDGLEY, SARAH, and VIRGINIA RICE, eds. *Terrorism, and the Media in the 1980's.* Washington, D.C.: Media Institute, 1984.

228 MONACO, JAMES, ed. *Celebrity: The Media as Image Makers.* New York: Dell, 1978.

229 MOORE, FRAZIER, and FRANK KALUPA. *Public Relations: Principles, Cases and Problems.* 9th ed. Homewood, Ill.: Richard C. Irwin, 1985.

230 NAVASKY, VICTOR S. *Naming Names.* New York: Penguin, 1981.
        Vivid description of the House Un-American Activities Committee probe into the political lives of Hollywood employees during the McCarthy era. Lengthy argument about the ethics of scapegoating or even casting suspicion upon others during a time of duress. <CC/ED>

231 NEWTON, RAY. "Native Americans and the Mass Media." Paper presented at the annual meeting of the Western Social Science Association, Arizona State University, Tempe, May 1976. [ERIC: ED127087]
        Using testimony from numerous sources, the report describes growing resentment in the American Indian community of Anglo media misinterpretation and exploitation of Native American cultures and people. Criticism from Native American media (American Indian Press Association Navajo Times, Ramah Navajo Broadcasting Station, Wassaja) is presented as a counterbalance to the norm. <JC/ED>

232 NORDENSTRENG, KAARLE. *The Mass Media Declaration of Unesco.* Norwood, N.J.: Ablex, 1984.
        Examination of the UNESCO document of 1978 highlights the resulting international law of communications, which provides standards for mass media performance. The second section treats the profession of journalism and contains a chapter on professional codes of ethics. Diagrams compare national and international documents. <UN/ED>

233 O'KEEFE, G.J. "Political Malaise and Reliance on Media." *Journalism Quarterly* 57 (Spring 1980):122-28.

234 ORWELL, GEORGE. *1984*. New York: Mentor, 1948

235 PACKARD, VANCE. *The Hidden Persuaders*. New York: David McKay, 1957.
Chapter 23, "The Question of Morality," is particularly significant to an understanding of advertising manipulation on one level at deeper levels, mass media in general. <ED>

236 PHELAN, J.M. *Disenchantment: Meaning and Morality in the Media*. New York: Hastings House, 1980.
Proposes that a public philosophy be developed from the humanities that can address issues of new media technology and cultural autonomy. Protests against neglecting the theoretical foundations of ethics in favor of reducing the field to codes and professional exhortations. <CC/DE/ED>

237 _____. "International Law and Control of the Media: Terror Repression and the Alternatives." *Indiana Law Journal* 53 (Summer 1978):619-777.
Special issue: Legal aspects of media coverage of terrorism.

238 PHILIPS, KEVIN. "Busting Media Trusts." *Harpers* July 1977, 23-24.

239 POPE, DANIEL. *The Making of Modern Advertising*. New York: Basic Books, 1983.
Chapter 5 contains a particularly germane discussion of the ethics of persuasion. <ED>

240 POSTMAN, NEIL. "The Las Vegasizing of America: The Humanities and Electronic Entertainment." *Etc.* 39 (Fall 1982):263-72.

241 RAWLES, BETH. "The Media and Its Effects on Black Images." 1975. [ERIC: ED158300]
Available through ERIC. Movies, television, radio, and print media have reinforced racial prejudice, negative images, and black stereotypes in the United States. History of media stereotypes and their effect upon the industry is balanced with 1970s attempts at media

reform. Establishment of black movie and press industry, push for affirmative action, citizen action groups, and black media ownership are covered. <MAI/ED>

242 RIVERS, WILLIAM L., and MICHAEL J. NYLAN, eds. *Aspen Notebook on Government and the Media.* New York: Praeger, 1973.

243 RIVERS, WILLIAM, T. PETERSON, and J.W. JENSON. *The Mass Media and Modern Society.* San Francisco: Rinehart, 1971.

244 RIVERS, WILLIAM L., WILBUR SCHRAMM, and CLIFFORD G. CHRISTIANS. *Responsibility in Mass Communication.* 3d ed. New York: Harper & Row, 1980.
     The first edition was one of the first book-length systematic examinations of mass media ethics. The third edition reiterates the notion of social responsibility, analyzes truthfulness and fairness as the tests of such responsibility, and discusses ethnic minorities, pluralistic programming, and the responsibility for promoting change. <UN/ED>

245 ROBERTS, C.L. Attitudes and Media Use of the Moral Majority." *Journal of Broadcasting* 27 (Fall 1983):556-64.

246 RODMAN, GEORGE. *Mass Media Issues.* New York: Science Research Associates, 1981.

247 ROHHER, DANIEL M. *Mass Media, Freedom of Speech and Advertising: A Study in Communication Law.* Dubuque, Iowa: Kendall-Hunt, 1979.

248 ROTZOLL, KIM, and CLIFFORD G. CHRISTIANS. Advertising Agency Practitioners' Perceptions of Ethical Decision." *Journalism Quarterly* 57, no. 3 (1980):425-31.
     Responses of 123 employees of four advertising agencies (three large, one small) suggest that personnel typically follow the standard of "immediate consequences" when deciding how to act. Critical thinking disappears and decisions are rationalized. Because working as a team member is essential, the exercise of individual conscience becomes extremely difficult. <UN/ED>

249 ROTZOLL, KIM, JAMES HAEFNER, and CHARLES SANDAGE. *Advertising in Contemporary Society.* Columbus, Ohio: Grid, 1976.

Advertising's roots are placed in the worldview and market of classical liberalism. Much of the discussion of advertising ethics should be viewed in that context. Misunderstanding over advertising currently arises from a cultural shift toward neoliberalism. <CC/ED>

250   RUBIN, BERNARD. When Information Counts: Grading the Media. Lexington, Mass.: Lexington Books, 1986.
        When information is important, does the public rely on mediated information? Interlocking essays focus upon such related issues as the media as mythmaker's mass stereotyping, women and media objectivity, buzzwords used to divert attention, legitimization of gossip as news, television coverage of courtroom proceedings, and pandering to public craving for sensationalism. <PR/ED>

251   RUBIN, BERNARD, ed. *Questioning Media Ethics*. New York: Praeger, 1978.
        Anthology of general articles, which include discussions of the fairness doctrine, the third world, stereotyping of women, and small town journalism. Two unique chapters deal with the depiction of journalists in motion pictures. <CC/ED>

252   SCHILLER, DAN. An Historical Approach to Objectivity and Professionalism in American News Reporting." *Journal of Communication* 29, no. 4 (1979):46-57

253   ____. *Objectivity and the News*. Philadelphia: University of Pennsylvania Press, 1981.

254   SCHMID, ALEX P., and JANNY DE GRAFF. *Insurgent Terrorism and the Western News Media: An Exploratory Analysis with a Dutch Case Study*. Leiden, Holland: Dutch State University, 1980.

255   SCHMIDT, BENNO C., Jr. *Freedom of the Press vs. Public Access*. Westport, Conn.: Praeger, 1976.

256   SCHMUHL, ROBERT. *The Responsibilities of Journalism*. Notre Dame: University of Notre Dame Press, 1984.
        Papers and speeches from an important conference at Notre Dame University in which media professionals, journalism educators, and ethicists compared viewpoints. Introductory essay on the nature and history of responsibility. <CC/ED>

257 SCHNEIDER, KAREN, and MARC GUNTHER. "Those Newsroom Ethics Codes." *Columbia Journalism Review* 24, no. 2 (1985):52.

258 SCHORR, DANIEL. *Clearing the Air*. Boston: Houghton Mifflin, 1977.

259 SCHUDSON, MICHAEL. *Discovering the News*. New York: Basic Books, 1978.

260 SCHULTZ, Q.J. Professionalism in Advertising: The Origin of Ethical Codes." *Journal of Communication* 31 no. 2 (1981):64-71.
    Although Americans usually agree that the professionalization of occupations creates socially responsible individuals, advertising was professionalized to sanction its social status and legitimize its economic advantage. Advertising ethics codes derive from the traditional desire to create an ideology and image of public interest. <UN/ED>

261 SCHWARTZ, TONY. *Media the Second God*. Garden City, N.Y.: Anchor Books, 1983.
    The omniscience and omnipresence of mass media, if not their omnipotence, rival the nature and control of Deity. Author lists many notable examples for his claim, primarily drawn from television and radio. Approach is primarily descriptive, not prescriptive. <ED>

262 SHAW, DAVID. *Journalism Today: A Changing Press for a Changing America*. New York: Harper's College Press, 1977.
    A collection of analytic and editorial style articles by the media critic/reporter for the *Los Angeles Times*. Also an original essay by the author on obscenity in media. <UN/ED>

263 ____. *Press Watch*. New York: Macmillan, 1984.
    This book contains essays written by the media critic and published in the *Los Angeles Times*. The author reflects on various ethical dilemmas for the media including confidentiality, deception, prizes, and court coverage. <DE>

264 SIBBISON, JIM. "Publishing New Drugs--Can the Press Kick the Habit?" *Columbia Journalism Review* 24, no. 2 (1985):52.

265 SIEBERT, FRED, THEODORE PETERSON, and WILBUR SCHRAMM. *Four Theories of the Press*. Urbana: University of Illinois Press, 1956.

Authors each describe one of four theories of the press. In "Authoritarian," the oldest of the four, truth is conceived as the product not of the great mass of people but of a few wise people (Siebert). In "Libertarian," the right to truth is an inalienable right; the press is conceived of as a partner in the search for truth (Siebert). In "Social Responsibility," a descendant of the Libertarian view, the power and near monopoly position of the media impose on them an obligation to be socially responsible (Peterson). "Communist" is a collectivist variation on Authoritarian (Schramm). <ED>

266   SMITH, ANTHONY.   "Is Objectivity Obsolete?"   *Columbia Journalism Review* 19 (May-June 1980):61-65.

267   SWAIN, BRUCE M.   *Reporters' Ethics*.   Ames: Iowa State University Press, 1978.
        Chapters cover reporter conflicts of interest, privacy, freebies, personal and corporate codes of ethics. FCC notions of equal time and fairness are discussed. Ten codes of ethics and a bibliography are appended. <AU/RR/DLM/CC/ED>

268   TEPJLUK, V.M.   *The Social Responsibility of the Journalist*.   Moscow: Mysl', 1984.
        In Russian. One of the most significant Soviet treatments of media ethics. Chapter 4 on moral responsibility states the insufficiency and often impossibility of mere legal attempts at press regulation. Thus ethical norms are highly significant within the profession. <SS/ED>

269   TEXAS   CHRISTIAN   UNIVERSITY,   DEPARTMENT   OF JOURNALISM. *Proceedings of Crime Victims and the News Media: The Right to Privacy vs. the Right to Know*. Fort Worth: Texas Christian University, Department of Journalism, 1987.
        Includes "Television's Coverage of Crime Victims" by Jeff Greenfield and presentations by Ed Lambeth, Roy Peter Clark, David Anderson, Alex Burton, Jim Plante, and others on how crime victims are covered by news professionals. <TT/ED>

270   THOMPSON, JAMES C., Jr. "Journalistic Ethics: Some Probing by a Media Keeper." *Neiman Reports* Winter-Spring 1978, 7-16.
        The head of the Neiman Fellowship program at Harvard University attempts to define the major questions of journalistic ethics during the 1970's. <DLM/ED>

271   TOMPERT, HELLA, ed. *Ethik und kommunikation: Vom Ethos des Journalisten*. Stuttgart, Germany: Katholische Akademie, 1980. In German.

272   TRABER, MICHAEL, ed. *The Myth of the Information Revolution*. Newbury Park, Calif.: Sage, 1986.
      Ethical problems of third world communication from eleven authors' perspectives, five of whom represent third world countries. Topics include erosion of national sovereignty, communication satellites and the third world, leapfrogging the Industrial Revolution, and the challenge of alternative communication modes. Traber is editor of *Media Development*, a periodical that emphasizes third world development and related communication issues. <PR/ED>

273   UNITED NATIONS. *The New World Information and Communication Order: A Selective Bibliography*. New York: United Nations, 1984.
      Emphasizes books and articles that provide documentation, analysis, and commentary on issues of international communication, particularly those emphasizing debates in UNESCO about (1) the free flow of information, (2) dependency and communication, and (3) the new world information and communication order.

274   WRIGHTER, CARL P. *I Can Sell You Anything*. New York: Ballantine Books, 1972.

I D. JOURNALISM ETHICS

275   ADAMS, JULIAN. *Freedom and Ethics in the Press.* New York: Rosen Publishing Group, 1983.

276   ANDERSON, DAVID A., and PETER BENJAMINSON. "The Ethics of Investigative Reporting." In *Investigative Reporting.* Bloomington: Indiana University Press, 1976; 6-17.

    Two sections of the book focus upon (1) sources and records and (2) investigative techniques. The chapter on the day-to-day reporter's ethics suggests that a general rule is "get away with whatever you can." < UN/ED >

277   AULETTA, KEN. "Bribe, Seduce, Lie, Steal: Anything to Get the Story?" *More*, March 1977, 14-20.

278   BAILEY, CHARLES W. *Conflicts of Interest: A Matter of Journalistic Ethics.* New York: National News Council, 1984.

    In the last study commissioned by the National News Council before its 1984 termination, this distinguished journalist analyzes the nature of major conflicts of interest and suggests remedies. < UN/ED >

279   BARNEY, RALPH D., JOHN JAY BLACK, NORMAN G. VAN TUBERGAN, and SCOTT WHITLOW. "Journalism Ethics and Moral Development: An Early Exploration." Paper presented at

the thirtieth annual meting of the International Communication Association, Alcapulco, Mexico, 1980. [ERIC: ED188181]

280   BLACK, JAY.   "Moral Development and Belief Systems of Journalists." *Mass Comm Review* 6, no. 3 (1979):4-16.
Special Issue: Journalism ethics.

281   BLACKENBURG, WILLIAM B., and RUTH WALDEN. "Objectivity, Interpretation, and Economy in Reporting." *Journalism Quarterly* 54 (Autumn 1977):591-95.

282   BLEYER, WILLIARD G., ed.   *The Profession of Journalism.* Boston: Atlantic Monthly Press, 1918.
Early anthology of essays about the problems and issues of print journalism.   Contributers include H.L. Mencken, Oswald Garrison Villard, and Ralph Pulitzer. <Ed>

283   BOHERE, G.   *Ethical Standards in the Profession.*   Geneva: Journalists' International Labor Office, 1984.

284   BOVENTER, HERMANN.   *Ethik des Journalismus: Zur Philosophie der Medienkultur.*   Konstanz: Universtiatsverlag Konstanz Gmbh, 1984.
In German. Boventer's lectures at Bonn and Munich include highly theoretical material on, for example, "the hermeneutics of understanding," "the journalist in self-reflection," and "good and bad in journalism." This massive (506 pp.) volume is characteristic of the prolific and sophisticated author. <RR/ED>

285   BOYER, JOHN.   "How Editors View Objectivity." *Journalism Quarterly* 58 (Spring 1981):24-28.

286   BROGAN, PATRICK.   *Spiked: The Short Life and Death of the National News Council.* Dallas: Priority Press, 1985.
An analysis of why the National News Council expired.   The report is sponsored by the Twentieth Century Fund, which also sponsored the task force whose study originally led to the birth of the National News Council. <UN/ED>

287   BROWN, LEE.   *The Reluctant Reformation: On Criticizing the Press in America.* New York: David McKay Co., 1974.
Author argues that throughout the long history of journalism criticism in the United States, the press has been "slow to heed its

critics and reluctant to adopt the reforms that society constantly requires of its press." Contains several codes of ethics and a typology of press critics. <DLM/ED>

288 BUKRO, CASEY.   "The SPJ Code's Double-Edged Sword: Accountability and Credibility." *Journal of Mass Media Ethics* 1, no. 1 (1985-86):10-13.

289 BULLETIN OF THE ASNE. "Journalism Ethics." *Bulletin of the ASNE*, October 1984, 4-17.
    A special section comprised of seven articles, primarily on ethical dilemmas facing reporters and news editors. Most the issues are germane to both television and newspaper coverage. <RR/ED>

290 CAPO, JAMES A.   "Limitations in the Traditional Code of Journalistic Responsibility."   Paper presented at the sixty-ninth annual meeting of the Association for Education in Journalism and Mass Communication, Corvallis, Oregon, 6-9 August 1983. [ERIC: ED237984]
    Objectivity, truth, freedom, and social responsibility--key principles in contemporary media ethics--fail to provide a practical, coherent code for responsible journalism.   In John Dewey's communication ethic, the fulfillment of these principles is ethical only to the extent that community empathy and foresight are enhanced. <MM/ED>

291 CAREY, JAMES W. "AEJ Presidential Address." *Journalism Quarterly* 55, no. 4 (1978):846-55.
    The growth of professionalism in news work has many problems worthy of criticism, according to the dean of the College of Communications at the University of Illinois at Urbana. <UN/ED>

292 CHRISTIANS, CLIFFORD G. "Beyond Quandaries: A Plea for Normative Ethics." *Mass Comm Review* 6, no. 3 (1979):27-31.
    Special Issue: Journalism Ethics.

293 ____. "Journalism Ethics in a Double Bind." *Ecquid Novi* 2, no. 2 (1981):61-68.
    Author claims that concerns for improving ethical awareness are being undermined by the press's unrelenting preoccupation with more technical skills and commitment to a "negative" view of freedom. <CC/ED>

294 CHRISTY, MARIAN. *Invasions of Privacy*: Note from a Celebrity Journalist. Reading, Mass.: Addison-Wesley, 1984.

295 CIRINO, ROBERT. *Don't Blame the People*. Los Angeles: Diversity Press, 1971.
   The author claims that the print and broadcast media must present all sides in public issues. Cirino writes: "Some may claim that the price of affording all viewpoints equal access. . . would be so expensive as to be impossible. But should price. . . .determine the picture we get of what's happening in the world?" <DLM/ED>

296 COMMISSION ON THE FREEDOM OF THE PRESS. *A Free and Responsible* Press. Hutchins Commission Report. Chicago: University of Chicago Press, 1947.
   The general report by the commission chaired by Robert Hutchins and financed by Henry Luce. Five requirements for a socially responsible press are outlined. <CC>

297 CORRIGAN, DON. "The Janet Cook Tragedy: A Lesson for Journalism Education." *Journalism Education* 36, no. 3 (1981):8-10.

298 COSTELLO, JAN R. "Exploiting Grief, Restraint and the Right to Know: Ethics and the Media." *Commonweal* 113, (6 June 1986):44

299 CRAWFORD, NELSON A. *The Ethics of Journalism*. New York: Alfred A. Knopf, 1924.
   First major U.S. book on journalism ethics. Commentary on unethical press practices and attempt to stimulate formation of professional codes in journalism. <CC/ED>

300 CURRY, J.L. *Press Control around the World*. New York: Praeger, 1982.

301 DAVENPORT, LUCINDA D., and RALPH S. IZARD. "Restrictive Policies of the Mass Media." *Journal of Mass Media* 1, no. 1 (1985-6):4-9.

302 DAVIS, ELMER. "News and the Whole Truth." *Atlantic Monthly*, August 1952, 32-38.

303 DEMOTT, JOHN. *The Ethics of Professional Journalism: An Annotated Bibliography of Suggested Readings*. Memphis: Society of Professional Journalists, 1980.

304   DENNIS, E. E. "The Press and the Public Interest: A Definitional Dilemma." *DePaul Law Review* 23 (Spring, 1974):937-60.

Surveys definitions of public interest, especially that of Virginia Held's, and asks whether public interest and the interest of the press are the same. Traces the emergence of a public interest doctrine in American law that gives the press relief from damages in such areas as libel. Finally, proposes a model for reconciling the two.

305   ____. "The Rhetoric and Reality of Representation: A Legal Basis for Press Freedom and Minority Rights." In *Small Voices and Great Trumpets: Minorities and the Media.* Edited by B. Rubin. New York: Praeger, 1980, 67-88.

Considers minority criticism of the press in order to ask whether the press should accurately represent the society and its component parts (1) in terms of the representativeness of news content, (2) in terms of newsroom personnel, and (3) in terms of the press as a representative of the public. Argues for a constitutionally based mandate for the press to provide a full picture to the minority communities. Press freedom is a personal constitutional right that cannot be enjoyed by most people unless there is a full and responsive press to channel information.

306   DENNIS, E.E., and A. ISMACH. "Representational Realities. In *Reporting Processes and Practices.* Belmont, Calif.: Wadsworth, 304-7.

307   DOIG, IVAN, and CAROL DOIG. *News: A Consumer's Guide.* Englewood Cliffs, N.J. Prentice-Hall, 1972.

Consumers are given tips on how to tell when a report is biased, how to spot hoaxes and public relations ploys, and how to conduct research with personal source notes. Other subjects include news critics, economics and ethics of the newsroom, and the endless contest among politicians, news professionals, and consumers. <HOD/ED>

308   EASON, DAVID L. "On Journalistic Authority: The Janet Cooke Scandal." *Critical Studies in Mass Communication* 3, no. 4 (1986):429-47.

309   EDWARDS, VERNE E., Jr.   *Journalism in a Free Society.*
      Dubuque, Iowa: W.C. Brown Co., 1970.
          Functions and status of the fourth estate are described for both
      broadcast and print journalism.   Appended material includes
      journalistic codes of ethics, magazine circulation statistics, sample
      stylebook, and sample headline schedule.   <SH/ED>

310   ELLIOTT, DENISE T., ed.   *Responsible Journalism.*   Beverly Hills,
      Calif. Sage, 1986.
          In opening chapters, Elliott and Hodges introduce and define
      notions of press responsibility.   Other contributors (Barney, Christians,
      Dennis, Glasser, Linsky, Merrill, Ziff) then examine specific tributaries
      and applications such as First Amendment values, representation, and
      pluralistic societies. Extensive bibliography.   <CC/ED>

311   EPSTEIN, EDWARD J.   "Journalism and Truth."   *Commentary* 57,
      no. 4 (1974):36-40.
          Applies Walter Lippman's ideas to several news gathering
      examples to demonstrate that the press cannot present the whole truth.
      Constrained by deadlines, confidentiality, economics, the press can do
      no more than signal an event.   <CC/ED>

312   FEDLER, FRED.   "Checkbook Journalism Proliferates, Harms
      both Public and Media." *Mass Comm Review* 7, no. 2 (1980):10-13.
          A review of several well-known examples of print and
      broadcast controversies.   In each, news organizations pay newsmakers
      for the privilege of exclusive coverage of a news event.   <DLM/ED>

313   FISHMAN, MARK.   *Manufacturing the News.*   Austin: University of
      Texas, 1980.

314   FITZGERALD, MARK.   "To Junket or Not to Junket?"   *Editor and
      Publisher* 117 (25 February 1984):12.

315   FLINT, LEON WILSON.   *The Conscience of the Newspaper.*   New
      York: D. Appleton, 1925.
          Actual cases in reporting, editorials, and advertising followed
      by suggestions for handling related ethical issues.   Parts 2 and 3
      consider the broad scope of forces and difficulties inherent within
      newspaper institutional structure and purpose.   <CC/ED>

316   FRY, DONALD, ed.   *Believing the News.*   St. Petersburg, Fla.:
      Poynter Institute Ethics Center, 1985.

317   GANS, HERBERT.   "Objectivity, Values, and Ideology."   In *Deciding What's News*. New York: Vintage, 1979, 182-213.

318   GARCIA, ARTHUR. "Journalism Contests: Ethical or Corrupt?" *Communication World* 1, no. 8 (1984):22-24.

319   GERALD, J. EDWARD. *The Social Responsibility of the Press*. Minneapolis: University of Minnesota Press, 1963.

   One of the earlier works on responsibility to evaluate the mass media as a social institution. A review of media performance precedes a series of complex but substantive proposals for press reform. <CC/ED>

320   GIBBONS, WILLIAM FUTHEY. *Newspaper Ethics: A Discussion of Good Practice for Journalists*. Ann Arbor, Mich.:   Edward Brothers, 1926.

   Advocates that codes of ethics and professional organizations be formed similar to those in medicine and law. Gibbon's observations about professional practice lead him to raise important questions. Mimeographed text. <CC/ED>

321   GINSBERG, ALAN R. "At Issue. Secret Taping: A No-no for Nixon--but Okay for Reporters." *Columbia Journalism Review* 23 (July/August 1984):16-19.

322   GLASSER, THEODORE L. "Objectivity Precludes Responsibility." *Quill*, February 1984, 13-16.

323   ____. "On the Morality of Secretly Taped Interviews." *Neiman Reports* 39 (Spring 1985):17-20.

   Author challenges most of the arguments against reporters secretly taping news sources and develops a logic of justification for certain types of surreptitious taping. <ED>

324   GOLDSTEIN, TOM. *The News at Any Cost: How Journalists Compromise Their Ethics to Shape the News*. New York: Simon & Schuster, 1985.

   Drawing upon years of behind-the-scenes experience at the *New York Times*, the *Wall Street Journal*, and other significant "bird's-eye view" locations, the author recounts several questionable reporting practices (checkbook journalism, fictional sources and details, conflict of interest, and so on) with telling detail. <ED>

325   GOODWIN, H. EUGENE.   *Groping for Ethics in Journalism*. Ames: Iowa State University Press, 1983.
      Provides journalists with both problems and possible solutions. Major categories of discussion include conflicts of interest; freebies, junkets, and perks; relationship of reporters and their sources; deception, eavesdropping, and lawbreaking; shocking words and pictures; privacy; an journalists as citizens and human beings.   Each category features a detailed case study. <UN/ED>

326   GOULD, S. "Coors Brews the News." *Columbia Journalism Review* 13 (March 1975):17-29.

327   GROSS, GERALD. *The Responsibility of the Press*. New York: Fleet Publishing 1966.
      Anthology of thirty-one essays by working journalists who discuss problems of ethics encountered in the field, and their approaches to them.   Four articles relevant to broadcast journalism ethics include essays by Robert Sarnoff, Frank Stanton, and Frank Kelly, and Fred Friendly's famous letter of resignation as president of CBS News. <RR/DLM/ED>

328   GROTTA, G.L.   "News vs. Advertising: Does the Audience Perceive the Journalistic Distinction?" *Journalism Quarterly* 53 (August 1976):448-56.

329   HACKETT, ROBERT A. "Decline of a Paradigm?   Bias and Objectivity in News Media Studies." *Critical Studies in Mass Communication* 1 (September 1984):229-59.

330   HARTLEY, CRAIG.   "Photographers, Public View Practices." *News Photographer*, January 1982, 23-25, 41.

331   HEINE, WILLIAM C. *Journalism Ethics: A Case Book*. London, Ontario: University of Western Ontario Library, 1975.
      Twelve case studies gathered primarily from British and Ontario press councils with official government responses and legal opinions accompanying some.   Topics include advertising, privacy, photo sensationalism, secret documents, and scandal reportage. <CC/ED/DE>

332   HEMANUS, PERTTI. "Objectivity in News Transmission." *Journal of Communication* 26 (August 1976):102-7.

333 HENNING, ALBERT F. *Ethics and Practices in Journalism*. New York: Long & Smith, 1932.

Drawing on forty years of journalism experience, Henning concludes that moral duty is primarily to colleagues; hence press professionals are committed to peers. Written as classroom text. <CC/ED>

334 HENRY, WILLIAM A., III. "Journalism Under Fire." *Time*, 12 December 1983, 76-93.

Following a precipitous drop in the polls, only 13.7 percent of the U.S. population in 1983 had confidence in the press. Possible causes include perception of press as unwelcome intruder, inaccurate, invader of privacy, interfering agent in courtroom atmosphere, confrontational assailant of public figures, and increasingly arrogant. <CC/ED>

335 HOCKING, W.E. *Freedom of the Press: A Framework of Principle*. Commission on the Freedom of the Press report. Chicago: University of Chicago Press, 1947.

A member of the Commission on the Freedom of the Press argues that there are no rights without responsibilities. Speaks of "the moral right of a people to be well served by its press" and "a right of the public to be served with a substantial and honest basis of fact for its judgments of public affairs" (168-69). Quotes Supreme Court stance on press responsibility. <DE/ED>

336 HODGES, LOUIS. "The Journalist and Privacy." In *Social Responsibility: Journalism, Law, Medicine*. Lexington, Va.: Washington and Lee University, 1983, 5-19.

Defines the nature of privacy and outlines a set of guidelines by which the press can respect the privacy of such people as public officials, innocent victims of tragedy, sudden or temporary news "heroes," and relatives of the prominent. <CC/ED>

337 HOLMBERG, SUSAN. "The Protection and Licencing of Journalists: A Global Debate." *International Communication Bulletin* 22, nos. 1-2 (1987):21-29.

338 HOOK, SIDNEY. "All Is Not Fair in News Reporting." *Wall Street Journal*, 21 February 1985, 31, 33.

339 HULTENG, JOHN L. *The Messenger's Motives: Ethical Problems of the News Media*. 2d ed. New York: Harper & Row, 1983.

Hulteng surveys the standards by which today's media operate and then compares actual performance with these guidelines. Focuses on individual practitioners who write, edit, produce, and report in print and broadcasting. Issues include conflicts of interest, source protection, and photojournalism practice. <CC/ED>

340 _____. *Playing It Straight*. Chester, Conn.: Globe Pequot Press, 1981.

Analysis of the statement of principles of the American Society of Newspaper Editors. Principles include freedom of the press, fair play, impartiality, and responsibility. Several specific examples are given. <CC/ED>

341 HULTENG, JOHN L., and ROY PAUL NELSON. *The Fourth Estate: An Informal Appraisal of the News and Opinion Media.* 2d ed. New York: Harper & Row, 1983.

Explores the rights and responsibilities of a free press. Relevant chapters include consideration of weaknesses of the press, the objective/subjective reporting dilemma, newsroom ethics, the opinion and editorial function, advertising, and conflicting constitutional rights. <SH/ED>

342 ISAACS, NORMAN. *Untended Gates*. New York: Columbia University Press, 1986.

343 IZARD, RALPH S. "Issues in Journalistic Ethics." Paper presented to the spring meeting of the Association for Education in Journalism and Mass Communication, Columbia, Missouri, 1984.

A survey of more than a thousand members of the Society of Professional Journalists, Sigma Delta Chi, the Associated Press Managing Editors, and the Radio-Television News Directors Association finds that American journalists have achieved a degree of consensus on traditional ethical problems and major issues such as news judgment and techniques. <DLM/ED>

344 JAEHNIG, WALTER B. "Journalists and Terrorism: Captives of the Libertarian Tradition." *Indiana Law Journal.* 53 (Summer 1978):619-777.

Special issue: Legal aspects of media coverage of terrorism.

345 JOHNSTONE, J.W.C., E.J. SLAWSKI, and W.W. BOWEN. *The News People: A Social Portrait of American Journalists and their Work.* Urbana: University of Illinois Press, 1976.

346 _____. "The Professional Values of American Newsmen." *Public Opinion Quarterly*, 36, no. 4 (1972-73): 522-40

347 KIRSCH, J.W. "The Ethics of Going Public: Communicating through Mass Media". *American Behavioral Scientist* 26 no. 2 (1982): 251-64.
Examination of scientist/press relationship; argues that both must better understand the other if public is to be well informed. Author recommends that scientists not be naive when dealing with the press and that the press not be ignorant of subject matter. Negative feelings and public misinformation may be avoided. <UN/ED>

348 KOCHER, RENATE. "Bloodhounds or Missionaries: Role Definitions of German and British Journalists." *European Journal of Communication.* 1, no. 1 (1986):43-64.

349 KURIAN, G., ed. *World Press Encyclopedia: Facts on File.* New York: World Press, 1982.
Mini-chapter-length descriptions of the state of broadcast and print journalism in 180 countries.. Relevant topics include law, ethics, regulation, national attitudes toward foreign press coverage, scope of training and education of journalists, and related. <RR/ED>

350 LAMBETH, EDMUND. *Committed Journalism: An Ethics for the Profession.* Bloomington: Indiana University Press, 1986.
Drawing upon moral philosophers and political theory, the author argues for enduring principles (truth telling, justice, stewardship, humaneness, freedom) as the overarching framework for journalistic practice. <CC/ED>

351 LANGGUTH, A.J. "The Dilemmas of Being a Reporter." *Nation*, October 1982, 328-30.

352 LASHNER, MARILYN. "Privacy and the Public's Right to Know." *Journalism Quarterly* 53 (Winter 1976):679-88.

353 LEVERE, J. "Guidelines for Covering Terrorists Debated." *Editor and Publisher*, 3 December 1977, 15+.

354 LOGAN, ROBERT A. "Jefferson's and Madison's Legacy: The Death of the National News Council." *Journal of Media Ethics* 1, no. 1 (1985-86):68-75.

Author argues that there were well-grounded rationales behind those who felt its establishment was ill-advised. Their attitudes reflected the difference between Jefferson's and Madison's views on the place of information in society. <UN/ED>

355 MC COLLOCH, FRANK. *Drawing the Line: How Thirty-one Editors Solved Their Toughest Ethical Dilemmas.* Washington: American Society of Newspaper Editors Foundation, 1984.
Complication of thirty-one case studies written by editors who present their most troubling ethical dilemmas. A joint project of the American Society of Newspaper Editors and the Poynter Institute for Media Studies. <CC>

356 MC DONALD, DONALD. "Is Objectivity Possible?" *In Ethics and the Press.* Edited by J.C. Merrill and R.D. Barney. New York: Hastings House, 1975, 69-88.

357 MC INTYRE, JERILN S. "The Hutchins Commission's Search for a Moral Framework." *Journalism History* 6, no. 2 (1979):54-57+.
Underlying the Hutchins Commission attempt to choose internal or external press guidance were the traditional tensions between the notion of freedom of the press and press responsibility. The middle-ground framework ultimately adopted was the idea of press "accountability." <UN/ED>

358 ____. "Repositioning a Landmark: The Hutchins Commission and Freedom of the Press." *Critical Studies in Mass Communication* 4, no. 2 (1987):136-60.

359 MC KAY, ROBERT B. *Freedom of the Press and Freedom from the Press.* Queenstown, Md.: Aspen Institute Publications, 1982.

360 MENCHER, MELVIN. *News Reporting and Writing.* Dubuque, Iowa: Wm.C. Brown, 1987.

361 MERRILL, JOHN. *Existential Journalism.* New York: Hastings House, 1977.
Drawing upon existentialist philosophers, particularly Sartre, Jaspers, Camus, and Kierkegaard, the author creates a model of the committed journalist. <RR/ED>

362 ____. *Global Journalism, A Survey of the World's Mass Media.* New York: Longman, 1983.

The first section discusses seven subtopics within the wider scope of international mass media: propaganda, news agencies, international broadcasting, international information order, national images, news flow, and interaction between governments and the press. <RR/ED>

363 _____. "Governments and Press Control." New York: Gannett Center for Media Studies, 1987.
   Study consists of interviews with official representatives from fifty-eight countries. Investigates the inclination to control the press by numerous national governments. An "Inclination to Control" index score is developed for each country. <JM/ED>

364 _____. *The Imperative of Freedom: A Philosophy of Journalism Autonomy.* New York: Hastings House, 1974.
   Attempt to establish the philosophical roots of journalistic ethics in libertarian ideals. <CC>

365 _____. *On Journalism Ethics.* Columbia, Mo.: Freedom of Information Center Report, 1970, 12-15.
   Applies particularly the individualistic values of John Dewey and Bertrand Russell within the framework of journalism ethics. <RR/ED>

366 _____. "A Semantic Analysis of the SPJ/SDX Code of Ethics." *Mass Comm Review.* 9, no. 1 (1981-82):12-15.
   Criticizes the code as being vague, overgeneralized, pretentiously lofty, and almost meaningless. Merrill conducts a close textual analysis. <UN/ED>

367 MERRILL, JOHN, and RALPH BARNEY. *Ethics and the Press: Readings in Mass Media Morality.* New York: Hastings House, 1975.
   This collection of thirty-six articles about news ethics includes Merrill on ethics and journalism, E. Epstein on truth telling, P. Weaver on old and new journalism, C. Huntley on press arrogance, P. Clark on newspaper credibility, and N. Hentoff on television fairness. <TS/DLM/ED>

368 MERRILL, JOHN, and JACK S. ODELL. *Philosophy and Journalism.* New York: Longman, 1983.
   Individual chapters treat divisions of classical philosophy as pertinent to journalism. Logic, semantics, epistemology, morality,

axiology, rhetoric, political theory, and metaphysics are topics, although ethics is an assumed subtext particularly in discussion of truth and morality. <CC/ED>

369 MEYER, PHILIP. *Editors, Publishers and Newspaper Ethics: A Report to the American Society of Newspaper Editors.* Washington D.C.: American Society of Newspaper Editors, 1983.

Report of detailed research into publisher's attitudes toward ethics as compared with those of editors. Discovers four types of publishers--politician, partisan, statesman, absentee. Each type is analyzed according to stance toward specific issues and response to case studies. <CC/ED>

370 _____. *Ethical Journalism.* New York: Longman, 1987.

371 MILLER, ARTHUR R. "The Press and Privacy." *Current,* July 1978, 3-7.

372 MILLER, ARTHUR R., ed. *An Enemy of the People.* New York: Penguin, 1977.

Adaptation of Henrik Ibsen's play about a newspaper editor's conflicting loyalties. Powerful symbolic depiction of how truth is received in the marketplace if threatening or painful to the majority. Examines the borderline between publishing/broadcasting for the benefit versus the detriment of society. <CC/ED>

373 MOLLENHOFF, CLARK R. "An Epidemic of Arrogance." *Quill* 74, no. 10 (1986):24-29.

374 _____. *Investigative Reporting: From Courthouse to White House.* New York: Macmillan, 1981.

While emphasizing the techniques and values of vigorous investigative coverage, especially of government, the author gives equal consideration to the counterbalancing danger of overzealous news gathering. <RR/ED>

375 NATIONAL ETHICS COMMITTEE, SOCIETY OF PROFESSIONAL JOURNALISTS, SIGMA DELTA CHI. *Journalism Ethics Report.* Chicago: Society of Professional Journalists.

Annual issues contain numerous articles, columns, occasional codes. Newspaper-style format creates in each issue dozens of short features that are too numerous to list but germane to journalism ethics. Includes some codes and articles by professionals. <DE/ED>

376   NATIONAL NEWS COUNCIL. *After Jimmy's World: Tightening Up in Editing.* New York: National News Council, 1981.

377   _____. *In the Public Interest I (1973-1975).* Minneapolis: Silha Center Publications, 1975.
In the Public Interest II (1975-1978). Minneapolis: Silha Center Publications, 1978.
In the Public Interest III (1979-1983). Minneapolis: Silha Center Publications, 1983.
Supplement to In the Public Interest III (1983). Minneapolis: Silha Center Publications, 1983.

378   NEWFIELD, JACK. "The 'Truth' about Objectivity and the New Journalism" *In Liberating the Media.* Edited by C.C. Flippen. Washington, D.C.: Acropolis Books, 1974, 59-64.

379   PETERSON, THEODORE. "Social Responsibility Theory since the Hutchins Commission." *In Press Theory in the Liberal Tradition.* Edited by James W. Carey and Clifford G. Christians. Urbana: University of Illinois Press, forthcoming 1989.
     Demonstrates that thirty years after the Hutchins Commission, social responsibility theory is largely a slogan. Although it formed the context for developing the Freedom of Information Act, social responsibility has basically been reduced to slogans like "the public's right to know." <CC/ED>

380   PICARD, ROBERT G., and RHONDA S. SHEETS. "Terrorism and the News Media Research Bibliography." Mass Communication and Society Division, Association for Education in Journalism and Mass Communication, Photocopy, 1986.
     More than 450 entries without annotations list books, articles, book chapters, monographs, unpublished materials, government reports, and documents. The thirty-three pages of titles on terrorism and the media include several works on the sociology and geopolitical issues of terrorism per se and at least half include questions of media ethics. Current copy is available from Robert Picard, Mass Communication Division, Emerson College, 100 Beacon St., Boston, MA 02116. <ED>

381 POYNTER INSTITUTE FOR MEDIA STUDIES. *The Adversary Press.* St. Petersburg, Fla.: Poynter Institute, 1983
        Tests Michael O'Neill's thesis, as stated in his address to the American Society of Newspaper Editors, that the press has become so adversarial in its relationship with government that it threatens the democratic process. (The Poynter Institute was formerly the Modern Media Institute Ethics Center.)

382 ____. *Believing the News.* Edited by Roy Peter Clark. St. Petersburg, Fla.: Poynter Institute, 1985.

383 PRESS COUNCIL OF INDIA AND THE INDIA LAW INSTITUTE. *Violations of Journalistic Ethics and Public Taste.* Bombay, India: N.M. Tripathi Private, 1984.

384 RASKIN, A.H. *Covering Crime: How Much Press-Police Cooperation? How Little?* New York: National News Council, 1981.

385 ROSHCO, BERNARD. "Press Releases and Pulitzer Prizes: The Diverse Meanings of 'Objective' News." In *Newsmaking.* Chicago: University of Chicago Press, 1975, 38-57.

386 RYAN, MICHAEL, and DAVID L. MARTINSON. "Ethical Values, the Flow of Journalistic Information and Public Relations Persons." *Journalism Quarterly* 61, no. 1 (1984):27-34.

387 SAALBERG, HARVEY. "The Canons of Journalism: A Fifty Year Perspective." *Journalism Quarterly* 50, no. 4 (1973):731-47.
        Reviews the origins of the code of ethics adopted by the American Society of Newspaper Editors in 1923. Attempts to analyze the more recent influence of the code. <RR/ED>

388 SANDERS, KEITH, ed. "Roundtable Discussion--Ethics: State of the Art." *Mass Comm Review* 6, no. 3 (1979):32-45.
        Special issue: Journalism ethics. Includes spokespersons from key professions. Dean James Carey concludes that ethical concerns among academicians studying the professional fields are not that far apart. Edited transcript of forum-style discussion. <ED>

389 SCHILLER, DAN. "An Historical Approach to Objectivity and Professionalism in American News Reporting." *Journal of Communication* 29, no. 4 (1979):46-57.

390 _____. *Objectivity and the News.* Philadelphia: University of Pennsylvania Press, 1981.

391 SCHMIDT, BENNO C., Jr. *Freedom of the Press vs. Public Access.* Westport, Conn.: Praeger, 1976.

392 SCHMUHL, ROBERT. *The Responsibilities of Journalists.* Notre Dame: University of Notre Dame Press, 1984.
Papers and speeches from important conference at Notre Dame University in which media professionals, journalism educators, and ethicists compared veiwpoints. Introductory essay on the nature and history of responsibility. <CC/ED>

393 SCHNEIDER, KAREN, and MARC GUNTHER. "Those Newsroom Ethics Codes." *Columbia Journalism Review* 24, no. 2 (1985):52.

394 SCHUDSON, MICHAEL. *Discovering the News.* New York: Basic Books, 1978.

395 SHAW, DAVID. *Journalism Today: A Changing Press for a Changing America.* New York: Harper's College Press, 1977.
A collection of analytic and editorial-style articles by the media critic/reporter for the Los Angeles Times. Also contains an original essay on obscenity in media. <UN/ED>

396 _____. *Press Watch.* New York: Macmillan, 1984.
Contains essays by a media critic published in the *Los Angeles Times.* The author reflects on various ethical dilemmas for the media including confidentiality, deception, prizes, and court coverage. <DE>

397 SIBBISON, JIM. "Pushing New Drugs--Can the Press Kick the Habit?" *Columbia Journalism Review* 24, no. 2 (1985):52.

398 SIEBERT, FRED, THEODORE PETERSON, and WILBUR SCHRAMM. *Four Theories of the Press.* Urbana: University of Illinois Press, 1956.
Authors each describe one of four theories of the press. In "Authoritarian," the oldest of the four, truth is conceived as the product not of the great mass of people but of a few wise people (Siebert). In "Libertarian," the right to truth is an inalienable right; the press is conceived of as a partner in the search for truth (Siebert). In "Social Responsibility," a descendant of the Libertarian view, the power and

near monopoly position of the media impose on them an obligation to be socially responsible (Peterson). "Communist" is a collectivist variation on Authoritarian (Schramm). <ED>

399 SMITH, ANTHONY. "Is Objectivity Obsolete?" *Columbia Journalism Review* 19 (May-June 1980):61-65.

400 SWAIN, BRUCE M. *Reporter's Ethics.* Ames: Iowa State University Press, 1978,
     Chapters cover reporter conflicts of interest, source relationships, management conflicts of interest, privacy, freebies, personal and corporate codes of ethics. FCC notions of equal time and fairness are discussed. Ten codes of ethics and a bibliography are appended. <AU/RR/DLM/CC/ED>

401 TEPJLUK, V.M. *The Social Responsibility of the Journalist.* Moscow: Mysl', 1984.
     In Russian. One of the most significant Soviet treatments of media ethics. Chapter 4 on moral responsibility states the insufficiency and often impossibility of mere legal attempts at press regulation. Thus ethical norms are highly significant within the profession. <SS/ED>

402 TEXAS CHRISTIAN UNIVERSITY, DEPARTMENT OF JOURNALISM. *Proceedings of Crime Victims and the News Media: The Right to Privacy vs. the Right to Know.* Fort Worth: Texas Christian University, Department of Journalism, 1987.
     Includes "Television's Coverage of Crime Victims" by Jeff Greenfield and presentations by Ed Lambeth, Roy Peter Clark, David Anderson, Alex Burton, Jim Plante, and others on how crime victims are covered by news professionals. <TT/ED>

403 THOMPSON, JAMES C., Jr. "Journalistic Ethics: Some Probing by a Media Keeper." *Neiman Reports,* Winter-Spring, 1978, 7-16.
     The head of the Neiman Fellowship program at Harvard University attempts to define the major questions of journalistic ethics during the 1970's. <DLM/ED>

404 TOMPERT, HELLA, ed. *Ethik und Kommunikation: Vom Ethos des Journalisten.* Stuttgart, Germany: Katholische Akademie, 1980.
     In German. Most of the material addresses journalism as a social institution and confronts structural issues regarding ownership and obligation in a sophisticated way. Other topics include the best

religious way to influence the media. These are transcribed lectures from a conference on journalism ethics held in Stuttgart. <CC/ED>

405   TUCHMAN, G. *Making News: A Study in the Construction of Reality.* New York: Free Press, 1978.

406   ____. "Objectivity as Strategic Ritual: An Examination of Newsmen's Notions of Objectivity." *American Journal of Sociology* 77 (January 1972):660-70.

407   WHITLOW, S.S., and G.N. VAN TUBERGEN. "Patterns of Ethical Decisions among Investigative Reporters." *Mass Comm Review* 6. no. 1 (1978-79):2-9.
      The authors employed Q-methodology in this study of thirty-four reporters' ethical problems. Three types of reporters were identified, but all three groups expressed a similar willingness to be jailed to protect source confidentiality and strongly rejected diluting or ignoring a story for money. <UN/ED>

408   WULFEMEYER, TIM K. "The Use of Anonymous Sources and Related Ethical Concerns in Journalism: A Comparison of the Effects of the Janet Cooke/*Washington Post* Incident on the Policies and Practices of Large Newspapers and Television Stations." 1982. [ERIC: ED217416]
      Unpublished; available through ERIC. Survey of sixty-five newspaper editors and sixty-four television news directors was conducted to examine policies concerning unnamed sources and unattributed information in stories. Results indicated that 24 percent of the newspapers and stations had formal written policies and 71 percent had informal policies. Half claimed that the Janet Cook case had no real effect upon their news-gathering and reporting practices. <HTH/ED>

I E. EDUCATION: TEACHING MEDIA
ETHICS

409   ALTSCHULL, J. HERBERT.   "The Origins of Journalism
      Education: A Cross-National perspective." Paper presented at the
      sixty-sixth annual meeting of the Association for Education in
      Journalism and Mass Communication, Corvallis, Oregon, 6-9 August
      1983. [ERIC: ED241920]
              Differences in journalism education worldwide reflect differing
      political, economic, and social milieus. Third world countries, unwilling
      to choose between only U.S. or Soviet views, endorse their own notions
      of objectivity, fairness, and journalistic balance. They view the press
      and government, however, as partners in organizing public thinking,
      and these ethics are reflected in their teaching. <MM/ED>

410   BAUMGARTEN, ELIAS. "Ethics in the Academic Profession: A
      Socratic View." *Journal of Higher Education* 53, no. 3 (1982):282-95.

411   BECKER, LEE B., JEFFREY W. FRUIT, and SUSAN L.
      CAUDILL. *The Training and Hiring of Journalists in the United
      States.* Norwood, N.J.: Ablex, 1986.
              Offers insight into the higher education of the 15,000 to 20,000
      students with degrees in journalism and mass communication who have
      graduated in each of the last several years. Describes the process of
      their joining primary media professions within the United States.

Although the role of ethics in media education is not given a separate chapter, implications may be drawn from the sections called "Description of" and "Effects of" the U.S. training system. <PR/ED>

412   BOK, DEREK C. "Can Ethics Be Taught?" *Change*, October 1976, 26-30.

413   BRANTLINGER, PATRICK. "Mass Communication and Teachers of English." *College English* 37, no. 5 (1976):490-509.
        Contends that communications textbooks uncritically accept and teach conformity, political passivity, and acceptance of the status quo. What ethics and thinking inform communication education? <JH/ED>

414   CALLAHAN, DAN, and SISSELA BOK, eds. *The Teaching of Ethics in Higher Education*. Hastings-on-Hudson, N.Y.: Hastings Center, 1980.
        Monograph summarized results of extensive study, funded by Carnegie Foundation, of the teaching of professional ethics in schools of business, law, medicine, journalism, engineering, and public policy. <CC/ED>

415   CARTY, JAMES W., Jr. "Should J-Schools Teach Ethics?" *Journalism Educator* 33 (1978):8

417   ____. "Problem Solving in a Mass Media Course." *Communication Education* 28, no. 2 (1979):139-43.A four-level decision-making strategy is described that teaches more effective problem solving. The levels are (1) identification, (2) generation of possible solutions, (3) choosing an alternative, and (4) evaluation. <CC/ED>

418   ____. "Teaching Media Ethics." *WACC Journal* 26, no. 4 (1979):19-22.
        Summary of issues, problems, and techniques germane to teaching media ethics to students who see themselves as preprofessional within a larger liberal arts program. <CC/ED>

419   ____. "Variety of Approaches Used in Teaching Media Ethics." *Journalism Educator* 33, no. 1 (1978):3-8, 24.
        Report from journalism schools about courses in ethics. Sixty-seven courses are identified; teaching techniques and materials used are summarized. <CC>

420 CHRISTIANS, CLIFFORD G., and CATHARINE L. COVERT. *Teaching Ethics in Journalism Education.* Hastings-on-Hudson, N.Y.: Hastings Center, 1980.

Comprehensive review of ethics instruction. Major issues, curriculum materials, teaching techniques, course objectives, and the overall state of the art are explained. Monograph is part of Hastings Center series on professional ethics instruction in American higher education. <CC/ED>

421 CHURCHILL, LARRY R. "The Teaching of Ethics and Moral Values in Teaching: Some Contemporary Confusions." *Journal of Higher Education* 53, no. 3 (1982):296-306.

422 COOPER, THOMAS W. "Communication and Ethics: Informal and Formal Curricula." *Journal of Mass Media Ethics* 2, no.1 (1987):71-79.

Posits that more education comes by means of mass communication (informal curricula) than through classroom education *about* mass media (formal curricula). Cites numerous "absurd" ratios including statistics about media ethics taught at all levels of education, and proposes alternatives. <ED>

423 CORRIGON, DON. "The Janet Cook Tragedy: A Lesson for Journalism Education." *Journalism Educator* 36, no. 3 (1981):8-10.

424 ELLIOTT, DENISE T. "Toward the Development of a Model for Journalism Ethics Instruction." Ph.D. Diss., Harvard University, 1984.

Provides analysis of three methods for teaching journalism ethics. Develops a tri-foundational theory based on moral obligations to society, peers, and one's own self or vision. Includes field observations of leading teachers of media ethics. <CC/ED>

425 EVSLAGE, THOMAS. *The First Amendment: Free Speech and a Free Press: A Curriculum Guide for High School Teachers.* Iowa City: Quill and Scroll, University of Iowa.

426 FRANKENA, WILLIAM K. "Toward a Philosophy of Moral Education." *Harvard Educational Review* 28, no. 4 (1958):300-13.

427 GERBNER, GEORGE. *Liberal Education for the Telecommunication Age.* Washington: American Association for Higher Education, 1983.

428 GOLDMAN, MICHAEL. "On Moral Relativism, Advocacy, and Teaching Normative Ethics." *Teaching Philosophy* 4, no. 1 (January 1981):1-11.

429 GOUINLOCK, JAMES. "The Moral Value of Philosophic Education." *Teaching Philosophy* 3 (1979):37-49.

430 HEARN, THOMAS. "Moralism and the Teaching of Moral Philosophy." *Teaching Philosophy* 3 (1979):51-63.

431 HILLIARD, ROBERT. "Curriculum's Technology Lag, Curricula and Television Literacy." In *Technology and Education*. Washington, D.C.: Institute for Educational Leadership, 1981, pp. 241-47.
    Courses in mass media should be made a basic aspect of education at all levels, from elementary school through higher education. Television has become such an important factor in our culture that study of its influence and nature must be incorporated into education if a democratic society is to survive. <AU/PGD/ED>

432 HUNT, TODD. "Raising the Issue of Ethics through the Use of Scenarios." *Journalism Educator* 37, no. 1 (1982):55-58.
    Five scenarios are outlined, which the instructor may easily employ as cases within the case study approach to teaching journalism ethics. <DLM/ED>

433 KOCH, SUSAN. "Technology, Television, and Values." *English Journal* 63, no. 7 (1974):24-25.
    Teachers must develop an ethical perspective on the uses of technology and the current influence of television. <JH/ED>

434 LICHTENBERG, JUDITH. *Ethics, Truth, and the Media: A Model Course.* College Park, MD: Center for Philosophy and Public Policy, 1986.

435 MC BRIDE, DONALD L. "Resources for Teaching Media Management Ethics." *Journal of Mass Media Ethics* 2, no. 1 (48-49).

436 MILLER, RICHARD I. *Education in a Changing Society.* Washington: National Education Association, Project on the Instructional Program of the Public Schools, 1963. [ERIC: ED024656]

One of three volumes discussing recommendations made in *Schools for the Sixties,* the official report of the National Committee of the National Education Association project on instruction. Topics include "The Mass Media, Particularly Television," "Science and Technology," "Leisure Time," and "Urbanization." <SG/ED>

437 PHELAN, JOHN M. *Mediaworld: Programming the Public.* New York: Continuum, 1977.

438 POTTER, ROSEMARY L. "A Special Program of Events." *TV Week* 96, no. 5 (1979):36,42-43.
   A full week of lessons, including field trips and speakers, is outlined to teach intermediate-grade pupils to view television more critically and explore its implications. <SJL/ED>

439 POWERS, CHARLES W., and DAVID VOGEL. *Ethics in the Education of Business Managers.* Hastings-on-Hudson, N.Y.: Hastings Center, 1980.

440 PURPEL, DAVID, and KEVIN RYAN. "It Comes with the Territory: The Inevitability of Moral Education in the Schools." In *The Hidden Curriculum and Moral Education.* Edited by Henry A. Giroux and David Purpel. Berkeley: McCutchen Publishers, 1983.

441 RIORDEN, SISTER MARY. "Religious Education and the Media in the Elementary School." *Catholic Library World* 52, no. 10 (1981):433-36.
   Positive and negative effects of media in religious education is based on church documents, including the documents of Vatican II and after, and on the author's personal experience as an elementary school teacher. <AU/LLS/ED>

442 ROSEN, BERNARD, and ARTHUR L. CAPLAN. *Ethics in the Undergraduate Curriculum.* Hastings-on-Hudson, N.Y.: Hastings Center, 1980.
   Monograph in the series resulting from the Carnegie study of professional ethics instruction in American higher education. Surveys the materials and strategies for teaching professional ethics to undergraduates. <CC>

443 SCHORR, PHILIP. "Learning Ethics: The Search for an Ideal Model." *Public Administration Quarterly* 7, no. 3 (1983):323-45.

444 SCHWARZLOSE, R.A. "The Dilemma of Journalism Education: Do as I Say, Not as I Do." *Mass Comm Review* 6, no. 3 (1979):20-26. Special Issue: Journalism Ethics.

445 SLOAN, DOUGLAS. "The Teaching of Ethics in the American Undergraduate Curriculum." *Hastings Center Report*, December 1979, 21-41.

446 TEBBEL, JOHN. "Can Journalism Schools Improve the Press?" In *Readings in Mass Communication: Concepts and Issues in the Mass Media.* 2d ed. Edited by Michael Emery. Dubuque, Iowa: Wm. C. Brown, 1974.

447 WARWICK, DONALD P. *The Teaching of Ethics in the Social Sciences.* Hastings-on-Hudson, N.Y.: Hastings Center, 1980.

II. TELEVISION AND ETHICS

II A. PRACTICES, PROGRAMMING, AND TELEVISION'S PRESENCE IN SOCIETY

448 ADLER, RICHARD, ed. *Television as a Cultural Force.* New York: Praeger, 1976.

449 ALLEY, ROBERT S. *Television: Ethics for Hire?* Nashville: Abingdon Press, 1977.
     Interview with forty television directors, writers, actors, and producers about (1) common values, if any, held by industry personnel, (2) ethical values conveyed or attempted through specific programs, and (3) television's influence on public attitudes and morality. <RR/ED>

450 ALTHEIDE, DAVID L. *Media Power.* Rev. ed. Beverly Hills, Calif.: Sage, 1985.
     Focuses more upon television than most works about the media. Social impact of network news and prime-time programming is emphasized. The revised text reemphasizes the central theme of the previous edition--how media, as organizations, have developed their own techniques, logic, procedures, and rationales. <RR/ED>

451 ARISTIDES. "Sinning in Black and White," *American Scholar* 47 (Fall 1978):449-50.

452 BARNOUW, ERIK. *The Image Empire: A History of Broadcasting in the United States since 1953.* Oxford and New York: Oxford University Press, 1970.

453 ____. *Tube on Plenty: The Evolution of American Television.* Oxford and New York: Oxford University Press, 1975.

454 BERGER, ARTHUR ASA, ed. *Television as an Instrument of Terror: Essays on Media, Popular Culture and Everyday Life.* New Brunswick, N.J.: Transaction Books, 1979.
      In addition to television, the popular culture landscape includes comics, advertising, humor, foods, fads, and artifacts. In this context, ethical questions proceed more from the examination of basic assumptions about society and *popular culture* than from specific cases and individual professional/public relationships. <PR/ED>

455 ____. *Television in Society.* New Brunswick, N.J. : 1986.
      Includes discussions of larger ethical issues such as advertising's commercial reality and images of the police (section 1) and the impact of television violence, freedom of the press, and the values transmitted by television (section 2). <PR/ED>

456 BROWN, LES. *Television: The Business Behind the Box.* New York: Harcourt Brace Jovanovich, 1971.

457 CATER, DOUGLAS. *Television as a Social Force: New Approaches to Television Criticism.* Queenstown, Md: Aspen Institute Program on Communication and Society, 1975.

458 CHRISTIANS, CLIFFORD G., and ROBERT FORTNER. "The Media Gospel: An Essay Review." *Journal of Communication* 31, no. 2 (1981):190-99.
      An evaluation of four books about religious broadcasting with overall emphasis upon televised religion. Authors of books are Ben Armstrong, James F. Engle, Malcolm Muggeridge, and Virginia Stern Owens. <CC/ED>

459 COMSTOCK, GEORGE. *Television in America.* Newbury Park, Calif.: Sage, 1980.

Examines ethical possibilities of news (does it divert?) and entertainment (does it become "information" and thus misinformation?). Provides solid overview of what is known about television and its three decades of social impact. <PR/ED>

460 CONE, FAIRFAX M. *With All Its Faults.* Boston: Little, Brown, 1969.

461 CROWTHER, H. "Religious Hucksters on TV." *Humanist* 35 (November 1975):44.

462 CURRAN, CHARLES. *A Seamless Robe: Broadcasting Philosophy and Practice.* London: Collins, 1979.

463 DATES, J. "Race, Racial Attitudes, and Adolescent Perceptions of Black Television Characters." *Journal of Broadcasting* 24 (Fall 1980):549-60.

464 DAVIS, RICHARD H., and JAMES A. DAVIS. *TV's Image of the Elderly:* Lexington, Mass.: Lexington Books, 1986.
Examines impact of television on the older person, images of the elderly in diverse programming genres, and overall effects of such stereotypes on society. Provides guide for alternative programming *by* senior producers, hosts, and so on, and in-depth orientation to major issues as viewed by a gerontologist and an educator. <PR/ED>

465 FINN, PETER. "Developing Critical Television Viewing Skills." *Educational Forum* 44, no. 4 (1980):473-82.
Teachers should transform the pervasive influence of television into a tool for developing critical viewing and media literacy in schoolchildren. Such critical TV viewing skills *can* also contribute to the achievement of the more traditional goals of classroom instruction. <SK/ED>

466 FORE, W.F. "Manual for the People: Deprogramming Television." *Christianity and Crisis* 37 (2 May 1977):93-96.

467 FORTGANG, STEPHEN J. "Teachers vs. Sellers: The Modern Mismatch." *High School Journal* 64, no. 3 (1980):131-33.
Author argues that teachers and schools, seeking to develop rational and thoughtful citizens, are locked into a power struggle with television and its sponsors. Sponsors have direct stake in creating a

manipulable, consuming mentality in the U.S. public, whereas teachers work toward a more free-thinking individualism. <AU/SJL/ED>

468 FRIEDMANN, GEORGES. "Television and Cultural Democracy." *Communications* 10 (1967):122-34.

469 FRIENDLY, FRED W. *Due to Circumstances Beyond Our Control.* New York: Random House, 1967.

470 GALLUP, GEORGE, Jr. "Forecast for America." *Television and Families* 8, no. 1 (Winter 1985):11-17.
 Examines views of current U.S. teenage population regarding value traits and family-shared television viewing habits, as well as overall trends in society among the adult population. Also reported are finds of a national survey conducted to determine proportion of adults who view television with their children on a regular basis. <MBR>

471 GERBNER, GEORGE. "Television: The New State Religion?" *Etc.* 34 (June 1977):145-50.

472 GITLIN, TODD, ed. *Watching Television.* New York: Random House, 1986.
 Examines basic assumption of television as a presence in society: What is it? Why is it? What are the ethical implications of supplanting the authentic with the artificial? With universal and romantic self-image? Authors include Daniel Hallin, Ruth Rosen, Tom Engelhardt, Pat Aufderheide, Michael Sorkin, and Gitlin. <PR/ED>

473 GREENFIELD, J. "Boob Rubes." *Columbia Journalism Review* 14, (Spring 1975):16-17.

474 ____. "TV Is Not the World." *Columbia Journalism Review* 17 (May 1978):29-34.

475 GRIFFITH, THOMAS. "TV Examines Its Excesses." *Time,* 22 July 1985, 61.

476 GROSSBERG, LAWRENCE, and PAULA A. TREICHLER. "Intersections of Power: Criticism-Television-Gender." *Communication* 9, no. 3-4 (1987):273-88.
 Inspects critical literature on television and sexual difference. Challenges assumptions of gender as a given and places sex roles and

rules within context of historical and social construction.
<AU/CS/ED>

477 HACHTEN, WILLIAM A. "Policies and Performance of South
African Television." *Journal of Communication* 29, no. 3 (1979):62-
72.
During its first three years, the South African television
broadcasting policy has been characterized by a pro-government stance.
As programming is aimed at the white audience, questions concerning
both social and communication ethics arise. <PD/ED>

478 HARRIOTT, J.F.X. "Television, St. George or the Dragon?"
Journal of Moral Education 13, no. 3 (1984):147-52.

479 HAWKER, JAMES F. "Sharing Faith in a Technological Age."
Momentum 8, no. 1 (1977):3-11.
Television, by the mid-seventies, was and continues to be first
in fulfilling the most important societal needs, according to the author.
These needs focus upon the transmission of both positive and negative
culture. <MO/ED>

480 HORSEFIELD, PETER G. *Religious Television: The American
Experience.* New York: Longman, 1984.
Historical review of research about religious programming on
U.S. television. Seeks to answer the question "What is known to date
about the social power of television and its behavior influence when
employed in the service of a strongly ideological organization?"
<RR/ED>

481 IGNATIEFF, M. "Is Nothing Sacred? The Ethics of Television."
Daedalus 114, no. 4, (1985):57-78.

482 INSTITUTE FOR THE STUDY OF CONFLICT. *Television and
Conflict.* London: Institute for the Study of Conflict, 1978.

483 JOFFE, PHYLLIS. "Cable and the Poor: Are All Viewers Created
Equal?" *American Film* 7 (October 1981):25-28.

484 JOHNSON, NICHOLAS. *How to Talk Back To Your Television Set.*
New York: Bantam, 1970.
Stinging attack on television practices and audience feedback
inadequacies by a former FCC commissioner. Central focus is upon

methods for citizens to participate in the improvement of television. <CC/ED>

485   ____. "Test Pattern for Living." *Etc.* 31, no. 1 (1974):15-25.
       Central thesis claims that Americans are ruled by interlocking corporations. The consumer's life, *as televised,* is the only viable life presented by these corporations through advertising, programming, and practices. Is there a strong correlation between the messages preached by television and our worst social problems? Moreover, does television avoid presenting alternatives to the consumer society, thus denying the public a choice? <JK/ED>

486   JOURNALISM QUARTERLY. "Research in Brief." *Journalism Quarterly* 62, no. 2 (1985):338-403.
       Special compendium.

487   JOURNAL OF MORAL EDUCATION. "Television, Broadcasting, and Ethics." *Journal of Moral Education* 13, no. 3 (1984).
       Special issue: Television and broadcasting ethics (J.F.X. Harriott, guest editor). Issues covered include effects of children's programming, adult education, international influence, and general morality of broadcasting programming. Contains several significant book reviews and useful introductory bibliography. <ED>

488   KREILING, ALBERT. "Television in American Ideological Hopes and Fears." *Qualitative Sociology* 5, no. 3 (1982):199-223.
       Presents the Chicago School of social thought, characterized by hope for a great community fashioned through new media technologies. Using the rise of television after World War II as a focus, author examines themes related to the hope of technological abundance. The new middle class used television as both the agency for creating a community and the arena through which status groups struggle for public legitimacy. <UN.ED>

489   KROHN, F.B. "Language of Television Preachers: The Marketing of Religion." *Etc.* 38 (Spring 1981):51-63.

490   LAGANA, JOSEPH F., sand GEORGE IANNACONE. "Television: Travesty and Truth." *NASSP Bulletin* 61, no. 405 (1977):93-96.
       Argues against the effectiveness of a family viewing plan described in an earlier issue of this publication. Offers recommendations urging the Federal Communications Commission to

assume more of a social responsibility in regulating television. <IRT/ED>

491   LEAR, NORMAN. "Does Television Have the Courage to Pioneer a New Commercial Ethic?" *Television Quarterly* 21, no. 4 (1985):7-14.
        This edited speech by a writer/producer crusader for more humanistic programming was delivered at the Television and Ethics Conference in Boston, December 1984. Argues that writers, producers, directors, and executives must not surrender their moral judgment to mere ratings rewards. He challenges the industry community to make television a creative instrument "to teach, illuminate, and inspire." <TVQ/ED>

492   LEARY, JOHN E. "Television: The Anti-Wellness   Tool." *Health Education* 10, no. 5 (1979):16-18.
        Individual and social health is influenced by the pervasiveness of television in American society. A strong case is made toward proving that television interferes with desirable (healthy) attitudes toward nutrition, sexuality, exercise, nonviolence, and general human wellness. <LH/ED>

493   LEVINSON, RICHARD, and WILLIAM LINK. "A Crisis of Conscience." *TV Guide*, 3 December 1977, 6-12.

494   LOVE, ROBERT. "The Media: A Look at Television." Paper presented at the Mid-South Sociological Association, 1979.
        Specific values may determine individual feelings toward television. Value judgments of individuals determine which aspects of television are viewed as problematic. Position is supported by those theories based upon R. Weinberg's development of value-conflict perspective. Other theories used include Fuller and Myers's stages of a social problem, Ogburn's cultural lag theory, Cooley's primary and secondary relations, and Sutherland's differential association theory. <UN/ED>

495   MAITLAND, JOHN C. "Ethics and Cable Television." *Audiovisual Instruction* 18, no. 10 (1973):33.
        Author foresees the need for the community, including particularly the education community, to have foresight about the implications of increasing penetration by cable television. Suggested is the proper planning for an orderly integration of cable technology and curriculum to serve education needs. <AU/ED>

496 MANDER, JERRY. *Four Arguments for the Elimination of Television.* New York: Morrow, 1978.

Four essays assert that (1) our primary environment is no longer natural, but man-made, (2) corporations use television to create a demand for their products, (3) viewing television may be physiologically harmful, and (4) unique qualities of television as a communication medium reduce, restrict, and devalue its content. <RR/ED>

497 MARK, N. "TV Junketeers." *Columbia Journalism Review* 13, (July 1974):27-32.

498 MASSING, M. "Should Public Affairs Be the Networks' Private Domain?" *Columbia Journalism Review* 19 (May/June 1980):34-37

499 MEEHAN, EILEEN R. "Conceptualizing Culture as Commodity: The Problem of Television." *Critical Studies in Mass Communication* 3, no. 4 (1986):448.

500 MEYROWITZ, JOSHUA. *No Sense of Place: The Impact of Electronic Behavior on Social Behavior.* New York: Oxford University Press, 1986.

Multi-award-winning commentary on social and psychic effects of contemporary telecommunications. As much or more than Berger, Postman, and Gitlin, Meyrowitz is acclaimed, primarily on the basis of this book, as a leading post-McLuhan prophet of television's hidden impact. <ED>

501 MILLS, LYNN. "TV Exchange: TV, a Value Indicator." *Teacher* 93, no. 4 (1975):72-74.

In 1974 prime-time *school* television conducted a survey of teachers to determine what kinds of evening television programs would be most helpful in teaching. Programs that develop *values* were most requested. The subject of this article is the resulting strategy for utilizing programming to help students better understand moral values. <UN/ED>

502 MOORFOOT, REX. *Television in the Eighties: The Total Equation.* London: British Broadcasting Co., 1982.

503 MORISON, PATRICIA, HOPE KELLY, and HOWARD GARDNER. "Reasoning about the Realities on Televisions: A

Developmental Study." *Journal of Broadcasting* 25, (Summer 1981):229-420.

504 NADLER, ERIC. "Guiding TV to the Right: Inside America's Favorite Weekly (*TV Guide*)." *Mother Jones* 9 (April 1984):17-20.

505 NEGRINE, R., ed. *The Challenge of Cable Television.* Croom Helm, England: Beckenham, 1985.

506 NEUHAUS, C. "Praise the Lord on TV--the 700 Club." *Humanist* 38, (January 1978):6-7.

507 NEWCOMB, HORACE. Mystery: Order and Authority." *Journal of Popular Culture* 7 (Spring 1974):966-80.

508 ____. *Television: The Critical View.* Oxford University Press, 1976.

509 ____. *TV: The Most Popular Art.* New York: Anchor/Doubleday, 1974.
     Important attempt by scholar trained in literary criticism to evaluate television programming rigorously. Chapters seriously evaluate such genres as situation comedies, westerns, mysteries, soap operas, and adventure programs. Ethical considerations are present within an analysis of implied values.

510 OZERSKY, D. "Content Free Medium." *Etc.* 35 (March 1978):86-89.

511 ____. "Television: The Isolating Medium." *Etc.* 34 (March 1977):100-3.

512 PERLOFF, R.M. "Loneliness, Depression and the Uses of Television." *Journalism Quarterly* 60 (Summer 1983):352-56.

513 POINDEXTER, P.M., and C.A. STROMAN. "Blacks and Television: A Review of the Research Literature." *Journal of Broadcasting* 25 (Spring 1981):103-22.

514 POOL, ITHIEL DE SOLA. "The Changing Flow of Television." *Journal of Communication* 27 (Spring 1977):139-49.

515 POSTMAN, NEIL. *Amusing Ourselves to Death: Public Discourse in the Age of Show Business.* New York: Viking Penguin, 1985.

Explores how television has damaged language, cheapened meaning, and reduced substance to mere surface in society. <ED>

516　POWELL, JODY. "Ratings, Ratings, Ratings." *Washington Post*, 30 June 1985, 19-22.

517　POWELL, JON T., and MYLES P. BREEN. "The Personal and Social Contributions of Television as Perceived by College Students." Paper presented at the annual conference of the International Communication Association, Pheonix, Arizona, 1971. [ERIC: ED049602].

　　　Students in basic speech class formed a sample for opinion survey about personal and social uses of television. The sample's major criticisms of television were (1) political commercials discourage understanding of issues, (2) false standards are developed by advertising, (3) commercials arouse desire for unnecessary products, and (4) television offers an easy avenue of escape from responsibility. <JK/ED>

518　"Will SNG Ever Be Banned in Boston?" *RTNDA Communicator*, November 1985, 22-23.

　　　Author voices concern over potential legal, ethical, medical, and technical hazards of sustained use of SNG systems. Chief cameraman at a Boston television station, the author advocates more research on the questions he raises. <DLM/ED>

519　RAVAGE, J.W. "Not in the Quality Business: A Case Study of Contemporary Television." *Journal of Broadcasting* 21 (Winter 1977):47-60.

520　ROSENFIELD, JAMES H. "Values and Quality--Two Simple Keys to Strategy." *Vital Speeches* 49, no. 10 (1983):312-15.

　　　Author, who held various executive titles with CBS television, argues that successful companies, such as his employer, share a common denominator--the determination to lead every field they enter. Business values, quality, realistic vision, and clarity of purpose form the backbone of success. He argues that CBS is handicapped in obtaining these goals by wrongheaded, outdated, and unfair government regulation. <UN/ED>

521　ROSSMAN, J. "TV Critic Column: Is it Influential?" *Journal of Broadcasting* 19 (Fall 1975):401-11.

522   RUBIN, A.M.   "Directions in Television and Aging Research." *Journal of Broadcasting* 26 (Spring 1982):537-51.

523   RUSAN, FRANCILE.   "What You See Is What You Get: Cable TV and Community Control." *Yale Review of Law and Social Action* 2, no. 3 (1971):275-81.

524   SAYRE, N.   "Reflections on the Tube."   *Columbia Journalism Review* 19 (September/October 1980):29-35.

525   SCHALINSKE, THEO FRED.   "The Role of Television in the Life of the Aged Person." 1968. [ERIC: ED030074].
      Unpublished; available through ERIC. A survey of senior adults found that television's attractiveness was related to the subject's dependence, social and physical isolation, and routine. Subjects found that their value systems provided conflict between their endorsement of television and their depreciation of its depiction of reality. Older adults may use television in spite of the fact that programs are designed primarily for younger persons. <AU/LY/ED>

526   SCHER, S.N.   "Role of the Television Critic: Four Approaches." *Today's Speech* 22 (Summer 1974):1-6.

527   SCHLESINGER, P. "Television in Europe: Quality and Values in Time of Change." *Media Culture & Society* 8, no. 1 (1986):125-31.

528   SEGGAR, J.F.   "Imagery as Reflected through TV's Cracked Mirror." *Journal of Broadcasting* 19 (Summer 1975):297-99.

529   ____.   "Women's Imagery on TV: Feminist, Fair Maiden, Or Maid?" *Journal of Broadcasting* 19 (Summer 1975):289-94.

530   SIEPMANN, CHARLES A. "Ethics and the Mass Media: What Is Wrong with TV-and with Us." In *The Range of Ethics*. Edited by Harold H. Titus and Morris Keeton. New York: American Book Co., 1966, 268-77.

531   SLABY, RONALD, GARY QUARFORTH, and GENE MC CONNACHIE. "Television Violence and Its Sponsors." *Journal of Communication* 26, no. 1 (1976):88-96.

532   SLATER, D., and W.R. ELLIOTT. "Television's Influence of Social Reality." *Quarterly Journal Of Speech* 68 (Fall 1982):69-79.

533   SMITH, ROBERT RUTHERFORD. *Beyond the Wasteland: The Criticism of Broadcasting.* Falls Church, VA.: Speech Communication Association, 1976.

Encourages viewers/listeners to inspect broadcast media more critically. Issues within the industry include broadcast journalism, planning and evaluation of cable and pay-cable television services, social effects of broadcasting, and the primary focus of the book--the informed criticism of television and radio. <RB/ED>

534   SPARKES, VERNON. "TV across the Canadian Border: Does It Matter?" *Journal of Communication* 27 (Fall 1977):40-47.

535   STOLLER, DAVID. "The War between Cable and the Cities." *Channels* 2, no. 1 (1982):34-37.

536   STREETER, SANDRA KAY, et al. "Television and Human Values: A Case for Cooperation." *Journal of Home Economics* 74, no. 2 (1982):18-20.

Examines the interaction between television and the profession of home economics. The tension between the two, particularly television's impact upon families and upon home values, raises many challenges. <JOW/ED>

537   SULLIVAN, EDMUND V. "Mass Media and Religious Values." *Religious Education* 78, no. 1 (1983):13-24.

Television has given audiences visual access to many events otherwise unavailable. It has, however, turned public events into private one-to-one intimate encounters in which television controls how much of the public event is seen. The medium perpetuates such myths as that of progress in which the exploitation of nature and capitalism dominate. TV evangelists offer an intimate religion in which conservative theology is congruent with these economic and cultural myths. <UN/ED>

538   TAN, A.S. "Television Use and Social Stereotypes." *Journalism Quarterly* 59 (Spring 1982):119-22.

539   ____. "TV Role Models and Anticipated Social Interaction." *Journalism Quarterly* 59 (Winter 1982):654-56.

540 TELEVISION INFORMATION OFFICE AND THE ROPER ORGANIZATION. *America's Watching: Public Attitudes toward Television*. New York: Television Information Office, 1987.

Results of a recent Roper study of public perception of television programs and practices. Cites television as primary source of news, most credible source of news, and other exceptionally positive findings. Ethical questions, dimensions, and implications of survey findings seem conspicuously absent. <ED>

541 THORNTON, LEE R. "A Correlation Study of the Relationship between Human Values and Broadcast Television." *Dissertation Abstracts International* 37 (March 1977):5424; 9A>.

542 THURSTON, CAROL M. "Accountability in Broadcasting." *Journal of Communication* 28 (Summer 1978):112-18.

543 TUCHMAN, GAYE. "Mass Media Values." *Society* 14, no. 1 (1976):51-54.

Argues that contemporary television programming helps maintain the existing political, economic, and social systems by refusing to question basic American assumptions about social arrangements. For example status-quo sex roles and property acquisition. Mass media take these arrangements for granted.

544 TV GUIDE. "Violence on TV: Does It Affect Our Society?" *TV Guide*, 14 June 1985.

Special Issue: Television and Violence.

545 TWEEDLE, S.W. "Viewing the Bible Belt." *Journal of Popular Culture* 11 (Spring 1978):865-76.

546 VARIS, TAPIO. "The Influence of International Television: A Case Study." *Journal of Moral Education* 13, no. 3 (1984):173-82.

547 WAHL, D.F., and R. ROTH. "Television Images of Mental Illness: Results of a Metropolitan Washington Media Watch." *Journal of Broadcasting* 26 (Spring 1982):599-605.

548 WARNOCH, MARY. "Broadcasting Ethics: Some Neglected Issues." *Journal of Moral Education* 13, no. 3 (1984):168-72.

549   WATSON, MARY ANN. "Television Criticism in the Popular Press." *Critical Studies in Mass Communication* 2, no. 1 (1985):66-75.

Proceedings of a conference at the University of Michigan. Focuses upon the criticism of television programs by newspaper professionals such as reviewers and columnists. <CC/ED>

550   WEIGEL, RUSSELL H. "American Television and Conventionality." *Journal of Psychology* 94, no. 2 (1976):253-55.

Survey of seventy-one adult residents of a medium sized New England town suggests that conventional social attitudes and values are associated with increased viewing of television. Values considered included measuring of views toward sociopolitical, marital, and fundamentalist religious issues. <UN/ED>

551   WENHAM, BRIAN. "Broadcasting and the Moral Imperative: Patrolling the Perimeters." *Journal of Moral Education* 13, no. 3 (1984):160-67.

552   WILLIAMS, RAYMOND. *Television: Technology and Cultural Form.* New York: Schocken Books, 1975.

553   WRIGHT, J.L. "Focus on Television Criticism." *Journal of Popular Criticism* 7 (Spring 1974):887-94.

554   WURTZEL, ALAN, and STUART SURLIN. "Viewer Attitudes toward Television Advisory Warnings." *Journal of Broadcasting* 22, no.1 (1978):19-31.

Presents the results of a survey that attempted to determine viewer reaction to potentially offensive programming. The tasks were (1) to determine what television content is considered inappropriate or offensive by viewers and (2) to assess which methods should be used to alert viewers to such content. <STS/ED>

II B. ADVERTISING AND TELEVISION

555 ATKIN, CHARLES K. "Political Advertising Effects on Voters and Children." Paper presented at the annual meeting of the American Psychological Association, Washington, D.C., 3-7 September 1976. [ERIC: ED147200]

Examines the influence of political television commercials on voting behavior. New data are reported about the role of voter-oriented ads in the socialization of children to the political environment. Concludes that campaign advertising directed at adult voters may also contribute to children's political socialization. <AU/DB/ED>

556 BLECKMAN, R.K. "Savage Mind on Madison Avenue: A Structural Analysis of Television Advertising." *Etc.* 37 (Spring 1980):38-52.

557 BLUM, ALAN. "The Great Tobacco Ad Ban Debate." *Quill* 74, no. 11 (1986):17-28.

558 BURR, P.L., and R.M. BURR. "Television Advertising to Children: What Parents Are Saying about Government Control." *Journal of Advertising* 5, no. 4 (1976):37-41.

Survey of four hundred U.S. parents reveals that most have strong doubts about the honesty of television advertising aimed at children. Authors argue that both the idea of children's advertising and the methods employed are suspect. More federal legislation is advocated. <RR/ED>

559 CANTOR, J. "Modifying Children's Eating Habits through Television Ads: Effects of Humorous Appeals in a Field Setting." *Journal of Broadcasting* 25 (Winter 1981):37-47.

560 CHAPKO, MICHAEL K. "Black Ads Are Getting Blacker." *Journal of Communication* 26 (Fall 1976):179-84.

561 CHOATE, ROBERT B. *The Eleventh Commandment: Thou Shalt Not Covet My Child's Purse.* Washington D.C.: Council on Children, Media, and Merchandising, 1971. [ERIC: ED071409]
    In the transcript of an appeal before the Federal Trade Commission the author pleads for governmental action to restrain national advertisers from "unscrupulous and erroneous advertising pitches aimed at children." Calls for FTC, FDA, and FCC regulation. Lists fifty largest food companies and their advertising agencies. <MC/ED>

562 CHRISTIANS, CLIFFORD G. "The 1976 Campaign and TV Advertising." *Illinois Business Review* 33 (May 1976):6-8.
    An analysis of how political television advertising in U.S. presidential elections short circuits the democratic process. Specific proposals for reform within television practice are recommended. <CC/ED>

563 CHRISTIANS, CLIFFORD G., and KIM B. ROTZOLL. "Advertising Agencies Practitioners' Perceptions of Ethical Decisions." *Journalism Quarterly* 57, no. 3 (1977):425-31.

564 COOK, JIMMIE E. "I Can't Believe I Ate the Whole." *Elementary English* 51, no. 8 (1974):1158-61.
    Asserts that curricula and programs focused upon teaching children to analyze television commercials should be developed by schools. The author argues that children should learn to recognize advertisers' propaganda techniques. <JH/ED>

565 COOK, ZENA, et al. *Impact of Advertising: Implications for Consumer Education.* Washington, D.C.: Public Interest Economics Center 1978. [ERIC: ED162165]
    This report reviews and analyzes the effects of advertising upon consumer choice, national values, and life styles. Intended to aid

consumer educators and others in related fields. The report focuses on the implications of television advertising upon our social and political lives. <CSS/ED>

566 COURTNEY, ALICE E., and THOMAS W. WHIPPLE. "Women: Nine Reports on Role, Image, and Message--Women in TV Commercials." *Journal of Communication* 24, no. 2 (1974):110-18.

One of a collection of reports published in this issue that focus upon the differences between the televised image of women and their real existence. <CH/ED>

567 DONAHUE, T.R., L.L. HENKE, 2d, and T.P. MEYER. "Learning about Television Commercials: The Impact of Instructional Units on Children's Perceptions of Motive and Intent." *Journal of Broadcasting* 27 (Summer 1983):251-61.

568 DOUGHERTY, PHILIP H. "A Question Is Raised on Recruitment Ads." *New York Times* 17, July 1980, D13.

569 DURHAM, TAYLOR. "Information, Persuasion, and Control in Moral Appraisals of Advertising Strategy." *Journal of Business Ethics* 3, no. 3 (1984):173-80.

570 FRAZER, CHARLES F. "Values in Prime Time Alcoholic Beverage Commercials." Paper presented at the sixty-sixth annual meeting of the Association for Education in Journalism and Mass Communication, Corvallis, Oregon, 6-9 August 1983. [ERIC: ED108666]

Content analysis methods were employed to determine values in seventy-seven beer and wine TV commercials. Author determined that critics' claim that "advertising subverts traditional American values" is dubious since findings support thesis that commercials carry values already important to large percentage of population. <HTH/ED>

571 GORN, GERALD J., and MARVIN E. GOLDBERG. "Children's Reactions to Television Advertising for Toys." 1974 [ERIC: ED119817]

Unpublished; available through ERIC. Study of 133 eight-to ten-year-old boys, who were presented with low, moderate, or high expectancies of winning a toy. They were presented zero, one, or three repetitions of an ad for the toy. The higher the number of repetitions, the greater the persistence of subjects at an insoluble task to win the toy. <AU/GO/ED>

572   HSIA, H.J. "Audience Recall as a Tolerance Toward Television Commercial Breaks." *Journalism Quarterly* 51, (Spring 1974):96-101.

573   JARVIS, DENNIS J. "The Perceived Utility of the Content of Over-the-Counter Drug Commercials: A Uses and Gratifications Perspective." *Dissertation Abstracts International* 39 (October 1978):1903, 4A.

574   JOSLYN, R.A. "Content of Political Spot Ads." *Journalism Quarterly* 57 (Spring 1980):92-98.

575   KAVANAUGH, JOHN. "Capitalist Culture as a Religion and Education Formation System." *Religious Education* 78, no. 1 (1983):50-60.
      Shows impact of television, especially T V commercials, on the formation of values. Commercials promise fulfillment through consumption; products are personalized; family life and intimacy are trivialized. Educators must offer alternatives that give other images of identity, relationships, justice, human dignity, life priorities, and the full spectrum of human emotions. <UN/ED>

576   KEY, WILSON BRYAN. *The Clam-Plate Orgy: And Other Subliminals the Media Use to Manipulate Your Behavior* (1980). See entry 208.
      _____. *Media Sexploitation* (1976). See entry 209.
      _____. *Subliminal Seduction* (1972). See entry 210.

577   KIDD, VIRGINIA V. "Nothin Says Lovin' Like Something from a Commercial: A Critical Look at Interpersonal Communication in Commercials." Paper presented at the annual meeting of the Western Speech Communication Association, Seattle, Washington, 1983. [ERIC: ED243155]
      Author believes that television commercials are purveyors of prescribed appropriate behavior. They have taken over authority for acceptable style and morality. Advertising language implies that behavior other than that prescribed is not acceptable. <HOD/ED>

578   KOTTMAN, E. JOHN. "Toward an Understanding of Truth in Advertising," *Journalism Quarterly* 47 (Spring 1970):81-86.

579   KROHN, F.B. "Sixty-Minute Commercial Marketing Salvation." *Humanist* 41 (November-December 1980):26-31.

580 LIEBERT, DIANE E., JOYCE N. SPRAFKIN, ROBERT M. LIEBERT, and ELI A. RUBINSTEIN. "Effects of Television Commercial Disclaimers on Product Expectations of Children." *Journal of Communication* 27 (Winter 1977):118-24.

581 LUCAS, RICHARD JAY. "The Effects of Adult-Oriented Advertising on First, Second, and Third Grade Children across Socio-economic Bounds." Ph.D. Diss., University of Massachusetts, 1976. [ERIC: ED147904]
   After viewing a half-hour television program that included six commercials, 227 children were interviewed about their recall of the commercials and their attitudes toward them. Analysis of results indicated that the white middle-class children understood commercial intent significantly more often than the others and that they were skeptical of the commercials' truthfulness. <AU/GW/ED>

582 LULL, J.T. "Counteradvertising: Persuadibility of the Anti-Bayer TV Spot." *Journal of Broadcasting* 18 (Summer 1974):353-60.

583 ____. "Recognition of Female Stereotypes in TV Commercials." *Journalism Quarterly* 54 (Spring 1977):153-57.

584 MC CLAINE, HILARY. "Creative Iconoclasts Spurn Hard Sell." *Advertising Age* 13 December 1982, M10-11.
   Toru Kawasaki and Shigesato Itoi, creative iconoclasts of Japanese advertising, have both found new ways to reach a public that is still put off by the obvious hard-sell tactics of the West, but is nonetheless increasingly sophisticated. Itoi thinks that U.S. advertising is based on misperceived values and a forgetting of what is important. Understanding of a product's values is more important than brand reinforcement. <UN/ED>

585 MAMAY, PATRICIA D., and RICHARD L. SIMPSON. "Three Female Roles in Television Commercials." *Sex Roles: A Journal of Research* 7, no. 12 (1981):1223-32.
   An evaluation of female roles as portrayed by TV commercials in 1977 suggests a decline in the role of mother as moral socializer, a rise in self-indulgent consumer behavior among children, and exaggerated differentiation between generations and genders. <JCD/ED>

586 MANDER, JERRY. *Four Arguments for the Elimination of Advertising.* Urbana: University of Illinois, Department of Advertising, 1979.

587 MATTES, J., And J. CANTOR. "Enhancing Responses to Television Advertisements via the Transfer of Residual Arousal from Prior Programming." *Journal of Broadcasting* 26 (Spring 1982):553-66.

588 MEESE, MILAN D. "Editorial Advertising and the First Amendment." *Journal of Advertising* 17 (Fall 1983):417-26.

589 MELODY, WILLIAM H., and WENDY EHRLICH. "Children's TV Commercials: The Vanishing Policy Options." *Journal of Communication* 24 (Fall 1974):113-25.

590 MEYER, T.P., and A. HEXAMER. "Perceived Truth and Trust in Television Advertising among Mexican-American Adolescents: Socialization and Developmental Considerations." *Journal of Broadcasting* 25 (Spring 1981):139-53.

591 MOSCHIS, GEORGE P., and ROY L. MOORE. "A Longitudinal Study of Television Advertising Effects." *Journal of Consumer Research* 9, no. 3 (1982):279-86.
    Examined the short- and long-term effects of TV advertising on the development of specific consumption-related orientations in four areas: (1) consumer role perceptions, (2) normative consumer activities, (3) materialistic values, and (4) sex-role perceptions. When 683 U.S. students in the sixth through twelfth grades were examined, in a two-wave study, TV advertising appeared to affect the development of materialism and traditional sex roles, particularly in the absence of discussion with parents. <UN/ED>

592 PALMER, E.L. "Children's Understanding of Nutritional Information Presented in Breakfast Cereal Commercials." *Journal of Broadcasting* 25 (Summer 1981):295-301.

593 PASKOWSKI, MARIANNE. "The TV Code Is Dead, But The Memory Lingers On." *Marketing and Media Decisions* 18, no. 14 (1983):64-66, 135-38.
    In the year following suspension of the National Association of Broadcasters code, most network and advertising executives had not detected significant changes in taste standards for television commercials. Networks now had total responsibility for what was

broadcast. Commercial clearance process could now be more complicated without the code, since an agency had to deal with three network content editors. <UN/ED>

594 PATTERSON, THOMAS. "It's Not the Commercial; It's the Money." *Television Quarterly* 20, no. 1 (1983):73-83.

595 PENDLETON, JENNIFER. "Ads, Ethics Clash for Haskell Wexler." *Advertising Age* 57, no. 12 (1986):10.
Haskell Wexler, an Academy Award-winning cinematographer, is contemptuous of those in the advertising industry who abandon ethical standards in the drive to make profits. He believes that advertising creators should accept the responsibility that accompanies their powerful roles. A celebrated feature film director of photography and writer/director of controversial documentaries, Wexler also spends much time filming commercials. He admits that he has, on occasion, compromised these beliefs, yet he insists that ad creators can encourage honest, harmless ad presentations. <UN/ED>

596 POWELL, JON T. "Broadcast Advertising of Medical Products and Services: Its Regulation by Other Nations." *Federal Communications Bar Journal* 25, no. 2 (1972):144-75.

597 PRASAD, V. KANTI, T.R. RAO, and ANEES A. SHEIKH. "Mother vs. Commercial." *Journal of Communication* 28 (Winter 1978):91-96.

598 REID, L.N., and H.J. ROTFELD. "How Informative Are Ads on Children's TV Shows?" *Journalism Quarterly* 58 (Spring 1981):108-11.

599 REID, N.L. "Key Visuals as Correlates of Interest in TV Ads." *Journalism Quarterly* 56 (Winter 1979):865-68.

600 ROBERTSON, THOMAS S. "Parental Mediation of Television Advertising Effects." *Journal of Communication* 29 (Winter 1979):12-25.

601 SCHMELING, D.G., and C.E. WOTRING. "Agenda Setting Effects of Drug Abuse Public Service Ads." *Journalism Quarterly* 53 (Winter 1976):743-46.

602   SCHWARTZ, TONY. *The Responsive Chord.*   New York:
       Anchor/Doubleday, 1973.
           Author claims that successful commercials, whether for
       products or politicians, must "strike a responsive chord"--that is,
       subconsciously resonate at the hidden frequency of the viewer/listener.
       Many useful examples, including author's own award-winning ads, some
       for radio, but predominately for television. Strategies and ethics of
       viewer manipulation are revealed more than challenged. <ED>

603   SHARPE-PAINE, LINDA. "Children as Consumers: An Ethical
       Evaluation of Children's Advertising." *Business and Professional
       Ethics Journal* 3, nos. 3-4 (Spring/Summer 1984):119-69.

604   SHIPMAN, JOHN M., Jr. "Pressures on TV Programs: Coalition
       for Better Television's Case."   Freedom of Information Center,
       Columbia, MO., 1985. [ERIC: ED253904]
           In 1981, the conservative Coalition for Better Television
       threatened an economic boycott against advertisers who marketed their
       wares on programs that the coalition felt featured excessive sex and
       violence. The boycott threat was criticized for three reasons: (1) it
       amounted to censorship, since advertisement involves speech, (2) it
       affected innocent bystanders, such as employees of the products
       advertised, and (3) it precluded the right of television audiences to view
       what they choose. Although the threatened boycott never materialized
       there is evidence that sponsors and networks were highly aware of the
       coalition, and made efforts to reduce objectionable programming,
       making the boycott unnecessary. <UN/ED>

605   SIMPSON, M. "Does She or Doesn't She? Revisited: The Calvin
       Klein Jeans Ads." *Etc* 38 (Winter 1981):390-400.

606   SLINGER, PEG. "Television Commercials: Mirror and Symbol of
       Societal Values." *Religious Education* 78, no. 1 (1983):29-37.
           Discusses how TV commercials contradict messages of
       religious values. Commercials urge a minority of the global population
       to consume the majority of its resources, including many unnecessary
       products, while millions live in poverty.   To avoid commercial
       seduction, viewers should be more critical, examine persuasive devices
       employed by advertisers, and become more reflective about products
       and their images. <UN/ED>

607   STAAB, WALTER. "Let's Dump Inconsistency in Wildly Varied Standards for Rejecting TV Spots." *Advertising Age* 48, no. 17 (1977):71-72.
      Advertisers face the problem of rejection by individual stations. Currently, each station seems to have a subjective say in what is ethically and morally acceptable. Stations employ a double standard in that they accept programs almost unquestioningly from networks but screen spots from advertisers. Alternative relations between advertisers and stations are suggested. <UN/ED>

608   TAN, ALEXIS, S. "TV Beauty Ads and Role Expectations of Adolescent Female Viewers." *Journalism Quarterly* 56, no. 2 (1979):283-88.
      A study of the responses of fifty-six high school girls shows the cultivation effects of beauty-related TV commercials. Their perceptions of the importance of sex appeal, youth, and beauty to women in four different roles were influenced by the ads. <GT/ED>

609   TAYLOR, RALPH. "The Advertising Game: Insidious or Instructive?" *Business Today,* Winter 1977, 27-30.

610   TURK, PETER. "Children's Television Advertising: An Ethical Morass for Business and Government." *Journal of Advertising* 8, no. 1 (1979):4-8.
      Considers the confrontation between the Federal Trade Commission and marketers/broadcasters over the regulation of children's television advertising. The effects of ethical conduct upon public policy are analyzed. <AU/RL/ED>

611   WARD, SCOTT. "An Ad Ban Would Be Ineffective." *Quill* 74, no. 11 (1986):29-31.

612   WEIS, WILLIAM L., HORACE R. KORNEGAY, LEWIS C. SOLOMON, and LEO GREENLAND. "The Fiery Debate over Smoking at Work: The Moral Minefield of Cigarette Advertising." *Business and Society Review* 51 (Fall 1984):16-20.

II C. CHILDREN AND TELEVISION

613 ABEL, JOHN D. "Family Type Influences on Child Television Viewing." Paper presented at the annual meeting of the Speech Communications Association, Chicago, Illinois, 1972. [ERIC: ED072477]

The television program preferences of children as influenced by family type were examined in this study. To determine family types, a fourfold typology of family interaction patterns was used. The degrees of similarity between child/mother programming preferences were found to be different among the four family types. <AU/LG/ED>

614 ANDERSON, JAMES A. "Televised Values and Family Values: Teaching Receivership Skills to Elementary School Children." Paper presented at the sixty-fourth annual meeting of the Speech Communication Association, Minneapolis, Minnesota, 2-5 November 1978. [ERIC: ED165219]

A curricular development project aimed at developing television viewing skills has developed a curriculum for the middle school grades. The project assumes that children can use viewing, listening, reading, and analytical skills to modify medium, source, and message effects. They can learn value identification, judgment, and clarification. <TJ/ED>

615   ANDREAS, CAROL R. "War Toys and the Peace Movement." *Journal of Social Issues* 25, no. 1 (1969):83-100.

616   ATKIN, CHARLES.
_____. "Broadcast News Programming and the Child Audience." (1978).
       See entry 797.

_____. "Political Advertising Effects on Voters and Children." (1976). See Entry 555.

617   ATKIN, CHARLES, and GARY HEALD.   "The Content of Children's Toy and Food Commercials." *Journal of Communication* 27 (Winter 1977):107-14.

618   BAECHER, CHARLOTTE, et al.   "Early Childhood Consumer Education Materials Project." Mount Vernon, N.Y.: Consumers Union of the United States Educational Services Division, 1973. [ERIC: ED086631]
       The consumer instruction received by commercial television viewers must be astutely interpreted, particularly by children. This publication, one of a series of six, was designed to help parents and early childhood educators understand the child's developing consumer knowledge and attitudes. <AU/KSM/ED>

619   BANKS, SERMOUS, and RAJINDER GUPTA. "Television as a Dependent Variable, for a Change." Paper presented at the eighty-seventh annual meeting of the American Psychological Association, New York City, 1-5 September 1979. [ERIC: ED182029]
       A study finds that there is a positive relationship between a child's concern for her health and well-being and her volume of television viewing. Heavy viewing behavior is associated with hostility or detachment toward the parent. Based upon questionnaire data from 673 third-, fifth-, and seventh-graders. <AU/RH/ED>

620   BARAN, S.J.   "Prosocial and Antisocial Television Content and Modelling by High and Low Self-Esteem Children." *Journal of Broadcasting* 18 (Fall 1974):481-95.

621   BARTON, THOMAS. "Fighting for Their Lives: The Applicability of the Fairness Doctrine to Violence in Children's Television Programming." *West Virginia Law Review* 82, no. 2 (1979):285-98. [ERIC: EJ227854]

There is much in the content of children's programming that, although constitutionally protected, should be subject to the fairness doctrine. One side of an issue is often all that children are exposed to through TV series and commercials. <AU/IRT/ED>

622 BUSBY, L.J. "Defining the Sex-Role Standard in Network Children's Programs." *Journalism Quarterly* 51 (Winter 1974):690-96.

623 BYBEE, CARL, DANNY ROBINSON, and JOSEPH TURNOW. "Determinants of Parental Guidance of Children's Television Viewing for a Special Subgroup: Mass Media Scholars." *Journal of Broadcasting* 26, (Summer 1982):697-710.

624 CANTOR, J. "Modifying Children's Eating Habits through Television Ads: Effects of Humorous Appeal in a Field Setting." *Journal of Broadcasting* 25 (Winter 1981):37-47.

625 CHOATE, ROBERT B. "Oral Argument in Children's Television Proceeding." Washington, D.C.: Council on Children, Media, and Merchandising, 1973. [ERIC: ED091408]
    The author advocates banning commercials from Saturday and Sunday morning television and makes several other recommendations to reduce the hard sell of children's advertising and improve the quality of children's programming. The FCC could establish a children's TV broadcast center, a children's programming code, better research activity, and a better policy on public service announcements. It could also facilitate better consumer/advertiser educational interaction. <MC/ED>

626 CHRISTENSON, PETER G. "Children's Perceptions of Moral Themes in Television Drama." Paper presented at the annual meeting of the International Communication Association, Honolulu, 23-27 May 1985.
    To determine children's perceptions of underlying morals or messages in television drama, a study was conducted in which four early prime-time situation comedies were selected for viewing by fifteen children per program in kindergarten and first grade, fifteen children per program in the third and fourth grades, and eight children per program in the sixth grade.

627 COATES, B., and H.E. PUSSER. "Positive Reinforcement and Punishment in Sesame Street and Mister Rogers." *Journal of Broadcasting.* 19 (Spring 1975):143-51.

628 COLLINS, W. ANDREW. "Developmental Aspects of Understanding and Evaluating Television Content." Minneapolis: Institute of Child Development, 1973. [ERIC: ED075096]
    Age differences affect children's understanding and evaluation of television content, and such differences may be related to social behavior after watching television. One type of age-related change concerns the cognitive skills children must use to comprehend content. <KM/ED>

629 COMSTOCK, GEORGE, and ROBIN E. COBBEY. "Television and the Children of Ethnic Minorities." Paper presented at the sixty first annual meeting of the Association for Education in Journalism, Seattle, Washington, 13-16 August 1978. [ERIC: ED168002]
    The children of ethnic minorities appear to have a distinctive pattern in regard to television. The pattern is exemplified by a different orientation toward the medium, by differences in tastes and preferences, by atypical behavioral effects, and by different information needs. Minority children, however, share much with other children such as parental concern but limited parental control. <AU/ED>

630 COSGROVE, MICHAEL, and CURTIS W. MC INTYRE. "The Influence of "Mister Rogers' Neighborhood on Nursery School Children's Prosocial Behavior." Paper presented at the Biennial Southeastern Conference of the Society for Research in Child Development, Chapel Hill, North Carolina, 1974. [ERIC: ED097974]
    The impact of "Mister Rogers' Neighborhood" on nursery school children's prosocial behavior seems to be beneficial, according to this study. Younger children, however, do not obtain greater benefits than older children from network programming. <CS/ED>

631 COURTRIGHT, J.A., and S.J. BARAN. "Acquisition of Sexual Information by Young People." *Journalism Quarterly* 57 (Spring 1980):107-14.

632 DESMOND, R.J., and T.R. DONAHUE. "Role of the 1976 Televised Presidential Debates in the Political Socialization of Adolescents." *Communication Quarterly* 29 (Fall 1981):302-8.

633   DOMINICK, J.R.   "Children's Viewing of Crime Shows and Attitudes on Law Enforcement." *Journalism Quarterly* 51 (Spring 1974):5-12.

634   DONAHUE, T.R.   "Black Children's Perceptions of Favorite TV Characters as Models of Antisocial Behavior." *Journal of Broadcasting* 19 (Spring 1975):153-67.

635   ____. "Learning about Television Commercials: The Impact of Instructional Units on Children's Perceptions of Motive and Intent." *Journal of Broadcasting* 27 (Summer 1983):251-61.

636   DOOLITTLE, J., and R. PEPPER. "Children's TV and Content: 1974." *Journal of Broadcasting* 19 (Spring 1975):131-42.

637   DREW, D.G., and R.B. REEVES. "Children and Television News." *Journalism Quarterly* 57 (Spring 1980):45-54.

638   EASTMAN, H.A., and M.B. LISS.   "Ethnicity and Children's TV Preferences*." Journalism Quarterly* 57 (Summer 1980):277-80.

639   ____. "TV Preferences of Children from Four Parts of the U.S." *Journalism Quarterly* 57 (August 1980):488-91.

640   EGAN, L.M.   "Children's Viewing Patterns for Television News." *Journalism Quarterly* 55 (Summer 1978):337-42.

641   FABER, RONALD., RICHARD M. PERLOFF, and ROBERT P. HAWKINS.   "Antecedents of Children's Comprehension of Televisied Advertising." *Journal of Broadcasting* 26 (Spring 1982):576-84.

642   FELSENTHAL, NORMAN A. "Sesame Street: Socialization by Surrogate." Paper presented at the annual meeting of the Speech Communication Association, Chicago, 1974. [ERIC: ED105987]
       Examined in detail are portions of "Sesame Street" programs that contribute to children's learning of socially acceptable attitudes and behaviors. Included is a review of controversy surrounding the program's treatment of the socialization process of preschool television viewers. <CS/ED>

643   GAFFNEY, MAUREEN, ed.   Parents, Kids and TV." *Young Viewers Magazine* 6, no. 1 (1983). [ERIC: ED241010]

Three articles offer parents suggestions on how to make television a positive experience for their children.   An editorial introduces the themes basic to all the articles: type and amount of television viewing should be regulated by parents; parents should discuss television with their children; and parents must become aware of the differences in the way adults and children perceive television portrayals.

644   GANTZ, WALTER, and JONATHAN MASLAND. "Television as Babysitter." *Journalism Quarterly* 63, no. 6 (Autumn 1986):530-36.

645   GRAY, NAN, and SYLVIA SUNDERLIN, eds. "Children and TV: Television's Impact on the Child." 1967. [ERIC: ED013666]
       Unpublished anthology available through ERIC.   Authors include E. Christiansen, R. Garry, P. Witty, F. Breitenfeld, Jr., L. Hopkins, P. Swenson, A. Day, A. McIntyre, and R. Schickell. Topics include TV research, teaching television, children's educational TV, parents and television, public television, "the unguarded hours," and the overall impact of television. <UN/ED>

646   GROSS, L.S., and R.P. WALSH.   "Factors Affecting Parental Control over Children's Television Viewing: A Pilot Study." *Journal of Broadcasting* 24 (Summer 1980):411-19.

647   GUNTER, BARRIE. "Television as a Facilitator of Good Behavior Amongst Children."   *Journal of Moral Education* 13, no. 3 (1984):152-59.

648   HARRISON, ALTON, JR., and ELDON G. SCRIVEN. "TV and Youth: Literature and Research Reviewed." *Clearing House* 44, no. 2 (1969):82-90. [ERIC: EJ010223]

649   HAWKINS, ROBERT PARKER. "The Dimensional Structure of Children's Perceptions of Television Reality." Paper presented at the annual meeting of the International Communication Association, Portland, Oregon, 1976. [ERIC: ED120855]
       This research demonstrated that children's conceptions of television's reality are multidimensional.   Therefore, instead of assuming that perceived reality "acts and is acted on" in only one way, future research must take this cognitive complexity into account. Subjects of the study were 153 elementary schoolchildren in Wisconsin. <RB/ED>

650 HAYNES, R.B. "Children's Perceptions of Comic and Authentic Cartoon Violence." *Journal of Broadcasting* 22 (Winter 1978):63-70.

651 HEINTZ, ANN CHRISTINE, and ELIZABETH CONLEY. Testimony: Statements made at the National Congress of Parents and Teachers National Hearing on Television Violence," Chicago, 25 January 1977. [ERIC: ED141812]

   After establishing the need for a precise definition of *violence*, presenters recommend among other things, that parents discuss television programs and the related social issues with their children, and that they learn to abstract about violence in order to demystify it. <GW/ED>

652 HUR, K.K., and S.J. BARAN. "One-Parent Children's Identification with Television Characters and Parents." *Communication Quarterly* 27 (Summer 1979):31-36.

653 JAMES, N.C., and T.A. MC CAIN. "Television Games Preschool Children Play: Patterns, Themes, and Uses." *Journal of Broadcasting* 26 (Fall 1982):783-800.

654 JOHNSON, CHRISTOPHER. "The Standardized Childhood." *Today's Education* 70, no. 4 (1981):25-28.

   Television, advertising, and mass media in general have created a popular culture in which adolescents and children are taught to gain material gratification and group membership by fitting themselves into a preconceived mold. Those who fall short often develop feelings of inferiority and may become isolated. <JN/ED>

655 JOHNSON, NICHOLAS. "Beyond Sesame Street." *National Elementary Principal* 50, no. 5 (1971):6-13.

   Examines the quality of television programs designed for children and discusses the influences of such programs. Reform measures are suggested. <MF/ED>

656 JOURNAL OF BROADCASTING. "Research on Children and Television: Symposium." *Journal of Broadcasting* 25 (Fall 1981):327-45.

   Special issue: Children and Television.

657 KATZ, STAN J., and PAUL VESIN. *Children and the Media.* Los Angeles: Children's Institute International, 1986.

Proceedings of the first international conference held in Los Angeles, 6-8 May 1985, and cosponsored by the Centre International de L' Enfance in Paris and the Children's Institute International in Los Angeles. Included were experts in child psychiatry, psychology, social work, education, and so on. Scholars and specialists found overlap among disciplines and recommended cross-disciplinary teamwork. <AU/ED>

658 KUHMERKER, LISA. "Social Interaction and the Development of a Sense of Right and Wrong in Young Children." Paper presented at the annual meeting of the National Council for the Social Studies, Atlanta, Georgia 1975. [ERIC: ED114347]

Brief descriptions of recent research in early childhood moral development. Author concludes that since television is often the child's primary view of society, moral education in school must include guided discussion of information and misinformation from the medium. <AU/DE/ED>

659 LEIFER, AIMEE DORR. "How to Encourage Socially-Valued Behavior." Paper presented at the biennial meeting of the Society for Research in Child Development, Denver, Colorado, 1975. [ERIC: ED114175]

This study investigated the influence of structured children's programming on prosocial behavior. Fifty-three children were tested in four situations: (1) individual test on Piagetian tasks, (2) observation of social behavior in two structured tasks, (3) observation of natural social behavior in the day-care center, and (4) observation of videotape viewing habits. Findings and implications are discussed. <BRT/ED>

660 LOUGHLIN, M., and R.J. DESMOND. "Puerto Rican Children's Perceptions of Favorite Television Characters as Behavioral Models." *Journal of Broadcasting* 24, (Spring 1980):159-71.

661 ____. "Social Interaction in Advertising Directed to Children." *Journal of Broadcasting* 25 (Summer 1981):303-7.

662 LULL, JAMES. "Girls' Favorite TV Females." *Journalism Quarterly* 57 (Spring 1980):146-50.

663 MC GREGOR, MICHAEL A. "Assessing FCC Response to Report on Children and the Media: Atypical Development?" *Journalism Quarterly* 63 (Autumn 1986):481-87.

664 MELODY, WILLIAM H., and WENDY EHRLICH. "Children's TV Commercials: The Vanishing Policy Options." *Index to Journals in Speech Communication through 1979.* Fall 1975, 113-25.

665 MEYER, T.P., and A. HEXAMER. "Perceived Truth and Trust in Television Advertising among Mexican-American Adolescents: Socialization and Development Considerations." *Journal of Broadcasting* 25 (Spring 1981):139-53.

666 MEYER, TIMOTHY P. "Children's Perceptions of Justified/Unjustified and Fictional/Real Film Violence." *Journal of Broadcasting* 17, no. 3 (1973):321-32.

667 MORISON, PATRICIA, MARGARET MCCARTHY, and HOWARD GARDNER. "Exploring the Realities of TV with Children." *Journal of Broadcasting* 23 (Fall 1979):453-63.

668 MORRIS, NORMAN S. *Television's Child: The Impact of Television on Today's Children: What Parents Can Do about It.* Boston: Little, Brown, 1971.
     Based upon extensive series of interviews with psychiatrists, psychologists, educators, television executives, producers, performers, advertisers, parents, and children themselves. Explores the effect of television on a child's values, examines the relationship between violence on television and violent behavior in children, and calls for control over TV's effects to begin at home. <JY/ED>

669 MURRAY, JOHN P., OGUZ B. NAYMAN, and CHARLES K. ATKIN. "Television and the Child: A Comprehensive Research Bibliography." *Journal of Broadcasting* 16 (Winter 1972):3-20.

670 NOLEN, LESLIE C. "Conceptions of Early Adolescents Regarding the Family Environment Depicted in Televised Family Programs and the Contribution of These Conceptions to Their Attitudes, Values, and Expectations Regarding Families." *Dissertation Abstracts International* 43, (1982):296, 1B.

671 PALMER, EDWARD, and AIMEE DORR. *Children and the Faces of Television: Teaching, Violence, Selling.* New York: Academic Press, 1980.

672 RAFFA, JEAN B. "Television and Values: Implications for Education." *Educational Forum* 49, no. 2 (Winter 1985):189-98.

Contains a summary of the prevailing concerns about the impact of television on the formation of values in youth and some resultant implications for curriculum and instruction. The article examines pre-emption of active daily play, spectatorship, deemphasis of the complexity of life, lack of creativity, speedy conflict resolution, and violence. <CT>

673 ____. "Values on Television Shows Watched by Elementary School Aged Children: The Development and Implementation of a Methodology." *Dissertation Abstracts International* 43 (1982):1830, 6A.

674 REEVES, B. and M.M. MILLER. "Multidimensional-dimensional measure of Children's Identification with Television Characters." *Journal of Broadcasting* 22 (Winter 1978):81-85.

675 REID, N.L., W.O. BEARDEN, and J.E. TEEL. "Family Income, TV Viewing and Children's Cereal Ratings." *Journalism Quarterly* 57 (Summer 1980):327-30.

676 REID, N.L., and C.F. FRAZER. "Children's Use of Television Commercials to Initiate Social Interaction in Family Viewing Situations." *Journal of Broadcasting* 24 (Spring 1980):149-58.

677 REID, N.L., and H.J. ROTFELD. "How Informative Are Ads on Children's TV Shows?" *Journalism Quarterly* 58 (Spring 1981):108-11.

678 ROBERTS, C. "Children's and Parents' Television Viewing and Perceptions of Violence." *Journalism Quarterly* 58 (Winter 1981):556-64.

679 ROSSITER, JOHN R., and THOMAS S. ROBERTSON. "Children's TV Commercials: Testing the Defenses." *Journal of Communication* 24 (Fall 1974):137-44.

680 RUBIN, A.M. "Child and Adolescent Television Use and Political Socialization." *Journalism Quarterly* 545 (Spring 1978):125-29.

681 ____. "Television Usage, Attitudes and Viewing Behaviors of Children and Adolescents." *Journal of Broadcasting* 21 (Summer 1977):355-69.

682 SANDELL, K.L., and D.H. OSTROFF. "Political Information Content and Children's Political Socialization." *Journal of Broadcasting* 25 (Winter 1981):49-59.

683 SHEIKH, ANEES A., and MARTIN MOLESKI. "Children's Perception of the Value of an Advertised Product." *Journal of Broadcasting* 21 (Summer 1977):347-54.

684 SHEIKH, ANEES A., V. KANTI PRASAD, and TANNIRU R. RAO. "Children's TV Commercials: A Review of Research." *Journal of Communication* 24 (Fall 1974):126-36.

685 SILVERMAN, L.T., and J.N. SPRAFKIN. "Effects of Sesame Street's Prosocial Spots on Cooperative Play between Young Children." *Journal of Broadcasting* 24 (Spring 1980):135-57.

686 SNOW, R.P. "How Children Interpret TV Violence in Play Context." *Journalism Quarterly* 51 (Spring 1974):13-21.

687 TIERNEY, JOAN D. *Parents, Adolescents, and Television: Culture, Learning, Influence: A Report to the Public. Summary of Findings. Research Report.* Ottawa: Canadian Radio/Television Commission, 1978. [ERIC: ED172763]
Findings of television research conducted in Montreal and Windsor, Canada, in February-May 1978. Parent-adolescent-television relationships, differences between ethnic and English families, differences in adolescent male and female values in program viewing, and the role of the family were important topics. Thirteen major findings are listed and discussed. <JD/ED>

688 _____. *Parents, Adolescents and Television.* Part 2. Ottawa: Canadian Radio/Television Commission, 1978.

689 ____. *Parents, Adolescents and Television.* Part 3, *Defining Ethnicity through Measurement Construct: A Cultural Perspective According to Harold B. Innis. Research Report."* Ottawa: Canadian Radio/Television Commission, 1979.
Study of ethnic and nonethnic adolescents and preadolescents and their families tested for perceptions of values by children and their parents in favorite television series viewed over a six-week period. An analysis of choices by value orientation is provided. <JEG/ED>

690 ____. "A Study of the Influence of Television Heroes on Adolescents: The Effects of Family Discussion of programs and Cross-Border, Intercultural, Hero Preference." *Communications* 9, no. 1 (1983):113-41.

Social values are perceived by adolescents through favored TV series, specifically through the thought and actions of heroes. Subjects from 240 families were drawn from culturally diverse populations from both sides of the U.S.-Canadian border. Family discussion style was measured for significant differences and effects: one group discussed programs with the child; the second did not discuss programs; in the third the child viewed alone.

691 TORNEY-PURTA, JUDITH. "The Values Learned in School: Policy and Practice in Industrialized Countries." *In National Commission on Excellence in Education.* Edited by John Schwille, 1982. [ERIC: ED227072]

A comparative analysis of values education in the United States, Germany, Japan, Great Britain, the Soviet Union, Sweden, and Canada analyzed eight assertions, one of which stated that television and other mass media have an important and often negative effect on young people's values. Recommends that coalition agendas be formed, that a description of values should be learned in schools, and that specific actions are needed to embody such values in daily education practice. <JD/ ED>

692 TUCKER, D.E., and J. SAFELLE. "Federal Communications Commission and the Regulation of Children's Television." *Journal of Broadcasting* 26 (Summer 1982):657-69.

693 TURK, PETER. "Children's Television Advertising: An Ethical Morass for Business and Government." *Journal of Advertising* 8, no. 1 (1979):4-8.

The confrontation between advertisers, broadcasters, and the Federal Trade Commission over regulation of children's television advertising is centered upon several ethical conflicts. First Amendment rights versus protection of children's innocence, capitulation to prohibition or censorship versus propagandistic tendencies among advertisers, and other tensions are examined. References. <UN/ED>

694 VERNA, M.E. "Female Image in Children's TV Commercials." *Journal of Broadcasting* 19 (Summer 1975):301-9.

695 WATTLETON, FAYE. "Truth or Consequences." *Television and Children* 6, no. 4 (1983):19-21.

Proposes changes in commercial television programming on human sexuality that would create a less confusing, healthier atmosphere for adolescents. Changes include more mature discussion of contraception, termination of sexual exploitation, illuminating joys and challenges of child rearing, and presenting positive family role modeling.

696 WEBSTER, J.G., and W.C. COSCARELLI. "Relative Appeal to Children of Adult vs. Children's Television Programming." *Journal of Broadcasting* 23 (Fall 1979):437-51.

697 WEIGEL, RUSSEL H., and RICHARD JESSOR. "Television and Adolescent Conventionality." *Public Opinion Quarterly* 37, no. 1 (1973):76-90.

Two independent questionnaire studies of high school and college youth investigated the degree to which psychological involvement with television is associated with conventional values, attitudes, and behaviors. The finding of both studies strongly suggest that involvement with television is associated with a syndrome of conventionality. <UN/ED>

II D. TELEVISION ENTERTAINMENT

698 ASANTE, M.K., and M.C. GONZALEZ. "Sex and Power on Daytime Television." *Journal of American Culture* 6, (Fall 1983):97-99.

699 BARBATSIS, G. "Soap Opera as Etiquette Book: Advice for Interpersonal Relationships." *Journal of American Culture* 6 (Fall 1983):88-91.

700 BAXTER, L.A., and S.J. KAPLAN. "Context Factors in the Analysis of Prosocial Behavior on Prime-Time Television." *Journal of Broadcasting* 27 (Winter 1983):25-36.

701 BLUMLER, JAY G. "Broadcasting Finance and Programme Quality: An International Review." *European Journal of Communication* 1 (September 1986):343-65.

702 BROWN, B. "Grant Tinker (Interview)." *American Film* 8 (September 1983):23-25.

703 BROWN, LEE. *The Reluctant Reformation: On Criticizing the Press in America.* New York: David McKay Co., 1974.
     Author argues that throughout the long history of journalism criticism in America, the press has been "slow to heed its critics and reluctant to adopt the reforms that society constantly requires of its

press." Appendix A contains special codes of ethics including some that apply to broadcast journalists. Appendix B lists the six main types of critics of American print and broadcast journalism. <DLM/ED>

704   BRYANT, J. "Appeal of Rough-and-Tumble Play in Televised Professional Sports." *Communication Quarterly* 29 (Fall 1981):256-62.

705   BRYSKI, BRUCE. "The 'De-Rhetorical' Function of Docudrama: A Generic Approach." Paper presented at the annual meeting of the Eastern Communication Association, Pittsburgh, 24-26 April 1981. [ERIC: ED203393]
      An increasingly popular form of mass media persuasion is the "docudrama," a hybrid of the informative documentary and the dramatic film. Docudrama distortion of history for dramatic effect raises serious ethical problems. The question that arises is at what point does a critic draw the line between "dramatic license" and "historical distortion"? <HTH/ED>

706   CANTOR, MURIEL G. *The Hollywood TV Producer, His Work and His Audience.* New Brunswick, N.J.: Transaction , 1987.
      Describes the constraints and rewards (and sometimes ethical conflicts) during the daily lives of television producers. Based on interviews with over eighty producers, which focused on whether a producer's institutional and individual employers influence decision making. <PR/ED>

707   ____. *Prime-Time Television: Content and Control.* Newbury Park, California: Sage, 1980.
      Describes the power struggle among producers, government, rating systems, unions, pressure groups, networks, and production companies to create prime-time television programs, including films later aired on television. Ethical choices are *implicitly* and legal constraints are *explicitly* discussed in the analysis of the program selection process. <PR/ED>

708   CAWELTI, J.G. "Some Reflections on the Videoculture of the Future." *Journal of Popular Culture* 7 (Spring 1974):990-1000.

709   CHESBRO, JAMES W., and CAROLINE D. HAMSHER. "Communication, Values, and TV Series." *Journal of Popular Culture* 8, no. 3 (1974):589-603.

Both the social values and the cultural images presented through television series influence human thought and behavior. How those values and images hold influence is the primary focus of this essay. <RB/ED>

710 CHRISTIANS, CLIFFORD G. "The Sensate in Sorokin and in Primetime Television." *Etc.* 38, no. 2 (1981):189-201.

Popular culture is viewed as a key factor in maintaining what Sorokin called a sensate worldview. Examples are given of how the transcendental is brought into film and television through such producers as Ozu, Bresson, and Dreyer. <CC>

711 COMPESI, R.J. "Gratifications of Daytime TV Serial Viewers." *Journalism Quarterly* 57, (Spring 1980):155-58.

712 COPPOLINO, JOSEPH S. "An Investigation of the Value Systems of Police and Nonpolice and Their Relationship to the Perception of Values and Events in One Episode of a Television Series about the Police." *Dissertation Abstracts International* 37 (1976):672; 2A.

713 COSBY, BILL. "Cosby Threatens to Walk Off Show over Apartheid Sign." *Jet*, 9 September 1985, 59.

714 DONAHUE, THOMAS. "Favorite TV Characters as Behavioral Models for the Emotionally Disturbed." *Journal of Broadcasting* 21 (Summer 1977):333-45.

715 DYER, WILLIAM G., and JEFFREY H. DYER. "The M*A*S*H Generation: Implications for Future Organizational Values." *Organizational Dynamics* 13, no. 1 (1984):69-79.

A survey of 1,082 college students showed that most thought their values and attitudes had been shaped by the television program "M*A*S*H." Most subjects thought that some of the people and practices in the program were representative of real-world organizations. Values emphasized by the "'M*A*S*H' culture" included trust in co-workers, engagement in meaningful activities, and recognition of individual competence. <UN/ED>

716 EDGERTON, G., and C. PRATT. "The Influence of the Paramount Decision on Network Television in America." *Quarterly Review of Film Studies* 8 (Summer 1983):9-23.

717 ELLIOTT, W.R., and D. SLATER. "Exposure, Experience, and Perceived TV Reality for Adolescents." *Journalism Quarterly* 57 (August 1980):409-14.

718 ELLIS, KATE. "Queen for One Day at a Time." *College English* 38, no. 8 (1977):775-81.
Explains the ways in which television situations exploit the feminist movement while simultaneously *containing* it. <DD/ED>

719 ENGLAND, DAVID A. "Television and Our Humanity." *English Journal* 74, no. 8 (December 1985):61-64.
Cites episodes from "The Bill Cosby Show, "Family Ties," and "Hill Street Blues" to suggest the humanizing potential of television.

720 ESTEP, R., and P.T. MAC DONALD. "How Prime-Time Crime Evolved on TV, 1976-1981." *Journalism Quarterly* 60 (Summer 1983):293-300.

721 FINZ, SHERRY D., and JUDITH WATERS. "An Analysis of Sex Role Stereotyping in Daytime Television Serials." 1975 [ERIC: ED137652]
Unpublished; available through ERIC. The verbal behavior of the characters of three daytime serials was analyzed over a period of two weeks of continual viewing. Coding included nineteen previously developed categories. Although popular and a *potentially strong socializing influence* on their audience, serials still present very few role models. <AU/ED>

722 FLANDER, JUDY. "Battlestar Los Angeles: The Networks Meet the Press." *Washington Journalism Review* 1, no. 8 (September-October 1979):57-60.
Television critic analyzes ethical challenges to reviewers and critics when networks offer plush junkets to attract such reporters to screenings of new programs, often with free trips, lodging, VIP treatment, and access to industry contacts. <AN/ED>

723 GANTZ, W. "Exploration of Viewing Motives and Behaviors Associated with Television Sports." *Journal of Broadcasting* 25 (Summer 1981):263-75.

724 GAULARD, JOAN M. "'Mary Hartman, Mary Hartman': An Analysis of Satire as a Violation of Soap Opera Stereotypes." Paper presented at the sixty second annual meeting of the Speech

Communication Association, San Francisco, 27-31 December 1976. [ERIC: ED137875]

The television program "Mary Hartman, Mary Hartman" was both a parody of the soap opera form and a satire on American consumer society. It intentionally revealed the social mythology that some viewed as oppressive to both men and women. <AU/AA/ED>

725 GITLIN, TODD. *Inside Prime Time.* New York: Random House, 1983.

Based on numerous interviews with network executives, this volume explains the frenetic pace, the unpredictable harvest, and the consequent ethical dilemmas associated with a tunnel vision industry. The only goal at the end of the tunnel is an elusive, often mirage-like carrot--"hit show." <PR/ED>

726 GOFF, DAVID H., LYNDA DYSART GOFF, and SARA KAY LEHRER. "Sex-Role Portrayals of Selected Female Television Characters." *Journal of Broadcasting* 24 (Fall 1980):467-78.

727 GOULD, CHRISTOPHER, DAGMAR C. STERN, and TIMOTHY DOW ADAMS. "TV's Distorted Vision of Poverty." *Communication Quarterly* 29 (Fall 1981):309-15.

728 GREENBERG, B.S., and C.E. WOTRING. "Sex on the Soap Operas: Afternoon Delight." *Journal of Communication* 31, no. 3 (1981):83-89.

Examines portrayal of intimate sexual behavior on soap operas and concludes that they have more sexual content than do prime-time programs and that the types of intimacies differ. Notes that soap operas are potentially a major force in the transmission of social values and sexual information to youthful viewers. <PD/ED>

729 ____. "Television Violence and Its Potential for Aggressive Driving Behavior." *Journal of Broadcasting* 18 (Fall 1974):473-80.

730 ____. "Three Seasons of Television Characters: A Demographic Analysis." *Journal of Broadcasting* 24 (Winter 1980):49-60.

731 HARDAWAY, FRANCINE. "The Language of Popular Culture: Daytime Television as a Transmitter of Values." *College English* 40, no. 5 (1979):517-21.

Demonstrates how five daytime television shows present specific American values. Money, materialism, shame, guilt, love, and sex are all analyzed. <DD/ED>

732 HAYNES, R.B. "Children's Perceptions of Comic and Authentic Cartoon Violence." *Journal of Broadcasting* 22 (Winter 1978):63-70.

733 HICKEY, NEIL. "Does TV Violence Affect Our Society?" *TV Guide*, 14 June 1976, 4-31.

734 HINTON, JAMES L., JOHN F. SEGGAR, HERBERT C. NORTHCOTT, and BRIAN F. FONTES. "Tokenism and Improving Imagery of Blacks in TV Drama and Comedy: 1973." *Journal of Broadcasting* 18 (Fall 1974):423-32.

735 HUR, K.K., and J.P. ROBINSON. "The Social Impact of 'Roots.'" *Journalism Quarterly* 55 (Spring):19-24.

736 JENSEN, LARRY, and MARK ZELIG. "Analyzing Value Content in Television Programs." 1979 [ERIC: ED179201]
    Unpublished; available through ERIC. Four prime-time television programs--"Charlie's Angels, "Little House on the Prairie," "Grizzly Adams," and "Lou Grant"--were rated by university students. Portrayal of moral reasoning and values were discussed within and between the programs. Differences in depicted values among the programs and apparent program trends are evaluated. <RAO/ED>

737 KAPLAN, S.J., and L.A. BAXTER. "Antisocial and Prosocial Behavior on Prime-Time TV." *Journalism Quarterly* 59 (August 1982):478-82.

738 KATZ, STEVEN, and ARTHUR NIKELLY. "The Impact of Television on Social Interest: An Adlerian Analysis." *Individual Psychology: Journal of Adlerian Theory, Research & Practice* 39, no. 1 (1983):78-82.
    TV conditioning functions primarily through the presentation of the ego or self-ideal, usually through dramatic characters. Common to most TV characters are the drive for superiority over others, inflated prestige, lack of sustained effort for the benefit of others, and an environment of instant excitement and mobility. However, these ego ideals contrast with the daily reality of factory, office, farm, and other workplaces. <UN/ED>

739 KREIZENBECK, A. "Soaps: Promiscuity, Adultery and 'New Improved Cheer.'" *Journal of Popular Culture* 17 (Fall 1983):175-81.

740 LECKENBY, J.D. "Attribution of Dogmatism to TV Characters." *Journalism Quarterly* 54 (Spring 1977):14-19.

741 ____. "Attribution to TV Characters and Opinion Change." *Journalism Quarterly* 58 (Summer 1981):241-47.

742 ____. "The Authoritarian Dimension of Entertainment Television." Paper presented at the annual meeting of the International Communication Association, Chicago, 25-29 April 1978.
    This paper reviews two studies concerning the authoritarian impact of entertainment television. The first study revealed a significant correlation between the authoritarianism of the viewer and the impact of the program. Results of both studies support the view that television can be used to legitimize the antisocial opinions of certain viewers. <MAI/ED>

743 LEMON, JUDITH. "Women and Blacks on Prime Time Television." *Journal of Communication* 27 (Fall 1977):70-79.

744 LONG, M.L., and R.J. SIMON. "Roles and Status of Women on Children and Family TV Programs." *Journalism Quarterly* 51 (Spring 1974):107-10.

745 LOUGHLIN, MEGAN, THOMAS R. DONAHUE, and WILLIAM B. GUDYKUNST. "Puerto Rican Children's Perceptions of Favorite Television Characters as Behavioral Models." *Journal of Broadcasting* 24 (Spring 1980):159-71.

746 LOWRY, D.T. "Alcohol Consumption Patterns and Consequences on Prime Time Network TV." *Journalism Quarterly* 58 (Spring 1981):3-8.

747 LOWRY, DENNIS T., GAIL LOVE, and MALCOLM KIRBY. "Sex on the Soap Operas: Patterns of Intimacy." *Journal of Communication* 31, no. 3 (1981):90-96.
    Assesses the extent and nature of sexual behavior in daytime soap operas. Concludes that they present a distorted picture of sexual behavior in America, particularly in the ratio of married to unmarried sexual behavior. Suggests that steady viewing may influence young viewers' attitudes and values. <PD/ED>

748 MC NEIL, JEAN C. "Feminism, Femininity, and the Television Series: A Content Analysis." *Journal of Broadcasting* 19 (Summer 1975):259-71.

749 ____. "Imagery of Women in TV Drama: Some Procedural and Interpretive Issues." *Journal of Broadcasting* 19 (Summer 1975):283-88.

750 ____. "Whose Values?" *Journal of Broadcasting* 19 (Summer 1975):295-9.
       Comments on an analysis of television portrayals of women by John F. Seggar. The key issue to McNeil is that television portrayals do not recognize the diversity of individual values but substitute sexual stereotypes. Discusses how feminists have actively sought to put pressure on networks to produce a wider scope of more realistic images of women. <UN/ED>

751 MARING, GERALD H. "Books to Counter TV Violence." *Reading Teacher* 32, no. 8 (1979):916-20.
       Comments upon nature and representativeness of violence seen on television by children. Presents a list of books with nonviolent themes that may be used as alternatives.

752 MIHEVC, NANCY T., et al. "The Censorship of 'Maude': A Case Study in the Social Construction of Reality." 1973. [ERIC: ED081055]
       Unpublished; available through ERIC. Censorship of the two-part television episode that dealt with abortion and vasectomy within the "Maude" series was socially informative. Two stations (WMBD in Peoria and WCIA in Champaign-Urbana) that chose not to air the episode received an increase in social status and the perception that stations may be autonomous in their right to exercise their view of reality. <CH/ED>

753 MOERAN, BRIAN. "Confucian Confusion: The Good, the Bad and the Noodle Western." In *The Anthropology of Evil.* Edited by David Parkin. New York: B. Blackwell, 1985, 92-109.
       Explains and discusses the ethics of Confucius as depicted on Japanese television. <AU/ED>

754 MONOCO, J. "Roots and Angels: U.S. Television 1976/77." *Sight and Sound* 46 (Summer 1977):159-61.

114

755 MORROW, LANCE. "The Politics of the Box Populi." *Time,* 11 June 1979, 95.

756 NEUHAUS, C. "Praise the Lord on TV--the 700 Club." *Humanist* 38 (January 1978):6-7.

757 NEWCOMB, HORACE. *TV: The Most Popular Art.* New York: Anchor/Doubleday, 1974.
    Important attempt by scholar trained in literary criticism to evaluate television entertainment programming seriously. Chapters discuss such genres as situation comedy, westerns, mysteries, soap operas, and adventure shows. <CC/ED>

758 NYSTROM, CHRISTINE L. "What Education Teaches about Sex." *Educational Leadership* 40, no. 6 (1983):20-25.
    On the one hand, parents and schools teach impulse control to teenagers. On the other hand, television says, "If you want it now, you should have it." <AU/ED>

759 ORME, FRANK, E. "Violence Is a Saleable Commodity." *Better Radio and Television* 13, no. 1 (1973. [ERIC: ED077185]
    Research by a Michigan State University team revealed industry attitudes that directly contradict either generally accepted television research methods or conventional ethical codes. Interviews with forty eight producers, writers, and directors indicated irresponsible attitudes concerning the effects of television crime programs. The research shows that television uses violence because it is a salable program commodity, despite the Nielsen statistics, well known by industry gatekeepers, showing that many children watch crime programs. <MC/ED>

760 PRISUTA, ROBERT H. "Televised Sports and Political Values." *Journal of Communication* 29, no. 1 (1979):94-102.
    Presents a study testing the hypothesis that more conservative values are a function of exposure to televised sports. Conservatism is used as a criterion variable to represent a composite score of other political values studies including authoritarianism, nationalism, egalitarianism, individualism, and sportsmanship. <JMF/ED>

761 RABINOWITZ, MARTIN S. "Violence Perception as a Function of Entertainment Value and TV Violence." *Psychonomic Science* 29, no. 6-A (1972):360-62.

Explores the relationship between children's violence perception and their previous exposure to television. Thirty-two female and twenty-one male fifth- and sixth-grade children were exposed to one of four television programs: violent/pleasing, violent/less pleasing, nonviolent/pleasing, and nonviolent/less pleasing. This finding supports a satisfaction interpretation of TV violence rather than the catharsis of familiarity explanation. <UN/ED>

762   RAINVILLE, R.E., and E. MC CORMICK. "Extent of Covert Racial Prejudice in Pro Football Announcer's Speech." *Journalism Quarterly* 54 (Spring 1977):20-26.

763   ROBERTS, CHURCHILL. "The Portrayal of Blacks on Network Television." *Journal of Communication* 15 (Winter 1970-71):45-53.

764   ROBINSON, B.E. "Family Experts on Television Talk Shows: Facts, Values, and Half-Truths." *Family Relations* 31, no. 3 (1982):359-78.

765   ROLOFF, M.E., and B.S. GREENBERG. "Sex Differences in Choice of Modes of Conflict Resolution in Real-Life Television." *Communication Quarterly* 27 (Summer 1979):3-12.

766   ROTHENBUHLER, ERIC W. "Media Events, Civil Religion, and Social Solidarity: The Living Room Celebration of the Olympic Games." *Dissertation Abstracts International* 46 (March 1986):2476; 9A.

767   SEGGAR, J.F. "Imagery of Women in Television Drama: 1974." *Journal of Broadcasting* 25 (Summer 1981):277-88.

768   SHAW, PATRICK W. "The Game TV Plays: Or, Why an English Teacher Came to Hate Barnaby Jones." [ERIC: ED133734]
      Unpublished; available through ERIC. One message of popular dramatic television programs during the 1970's is that if the hero is, or appears to be, stupid (such as Archie Bunker, Fred Sanford, Columbo), then corruption may be equated with wealth, education, and literacy. Conversely, virtue may be equated with poverty and even illiteracy. One subconscious message is that the articulate speaking of correct English is elitist and undesirable. <JM/ED>

769 SILVERMAN, THERESA L., JOYCE N. SPRAFKIN, and ELI A. RUBENSTEIN. "Physical Contact and Sexual Behavior on Prime-Time TV." *Journal of Communication* 29 (Winter 1979):33-43.

770 SKILL, T. "Television's Families: Real by Day, Ideal by Night?" *Journal of American Culture* 6 (Fall 1983):72-75.

771 SLABY, RONALD, G., GARY R. QUARFORTH, and GENE A. MC CONNACHIE. "Television Violence and Its Sponsors." *Journal of Communication* 26 (Winter 1976):88-96.

772 STEIN, H.F. "In Search of Roots: An Epic of Origins and Destiny." *Journal of Popular Culture* 11 (Summer 1977):11-17.

773 STOCKING, S. HOLLY, BARRY S. SAPOLSKY, and DOLF ZILLMAN. "Sex Discrimination in Prime Time Humor." *Journal of Broadcasting* 21 (Fall 1977):447-57.

774 STUTZMAN, BRENT. *Television's 'Soap' Controversy.* Columbia, Miss.: Freedom of Information Center, 1978. [ERIC: ED153278]
   The situation comedy "Soap," television's first prime-time sex farce, stirred controversy months before its premiere. Subsequent pressure on advertisers forced the network to change the program's concept from an adult comedy to a "whodunit." This report summarized the controversy, recounts reactions to the series, and lists ethical implications of the debate. <MAI/ED>

775 SULZER, ELMER G., and GEORGE C. JOHNSON. "Attitudes toward Deception in Television." *Journal of Broadcasting* 4, no. 2 (1960):97-109.
   Reports results of a survey taken immediately following the quiz show "fix" publicity at the end of television's first decade. Five selected groups recognized the rigging of television quiz programs and acceptance of payola by radio disk jockeys as morally wrong. <UN/ED>

776 SURLIN, S.H. "Roots Research: A Summary of Findings." *Journal of Broadcasting* 22 (Summer 1978):309-20.

777 SUTHERLAND, JOHN C., and SHELLY SINIAWSKY. "The Treatment and Resolution of Moral Violations on Soap Operas." *Journal of Communication* 32 (Spring 1982):67-74.

Suggests that criticisms concerning soap operas' effects on morals and ethics may not be totally warranted; research found that moral violations tended to be resolved consistently with traditional moral standards, at least according to episodes of "All My Children" and "General Hospital" as reported in the 1980 issues of *Soap Opera Digest*. <PD/ED>

778   TAIBBI, MIKE. "Hearing It All from Our Heroes: Sports Broadcasts." *New York Times,* 13 October 1985, sec. 5, 2.

779   TATE, EUGENE D., and STUART H. SURLIN. "A Cross-Cultural Comparison of Viewer Agreement with Opinionated Television Characters." 1975. [ERIC: ED106884]
    Unpublished; available through ERIC. Tests relationship between dogmatism and agreement with the dramatic character Archie Bunker among adult Canadians. Hypothesis: highly dogmatic Canadians would demonstrate the same identification with Archie that highly dogmatic U.S. viewers demonstrate. Second hypothesis: Canadians would not view "All in the Family" as being realistic, unlike U.S. viewers, since the program is not set in Canada. Both hypotheses were confirmed. <RB/ED>

780   THORPE, NORMAN. "Utahans Fight over Decency in Cable TV." *Wall Street Journal,* 23 September 1982, sec. 2, 35, 37.

781   THOVERON, GABRIEL. "European Televised Women." *European Journal of Communication,* 1, no. 3 (1986):289-300.

782   UNDERWOOD, JOHN. "Plague of Money Madness." *AGB Reports* 25, no. 6 (1983):34-36.
    Academics and athletics must be distinguished, and athletes' roles at various levels understood and accepted. Three negative elements of professional sports must be controlled on campuses: pressured coaching, recruiting, and the encroachment of television entertainment, which transforms sport to show business and athletes to (paid) celebrities. <MSE>

783   VENUTI, L. "Rod Serling, Television Censorship, The Twilight Zone." *Western Humanities Review* 35 (Winter 1981):354-66.

784   VOLGY, T.J., and J.E. SCHWARTZ. "TV Entertainment Programming and Sociopolitical Attitudes." *Journalism Quarterly* 57 (Spring 1980):150-55.

785   WANDER, J. "Counters in the Social Drama: Some Notes on 'All in the Family.'" *Journal of Popular Culture* 8 (Winter 1974):604-9.

786   WHALEY, A. BENNETT, EDMUND P. KAMINSKI, WILLIAM I. GORDEN, and D. RAY HEISEY. "Docudrama from Different Temporal Perspectives: Reactions to NBC's'Kent State.'" *Journal of Broadcasting* 27 (Summer 1983):285-89.

II E. TELEVISION NEWS

787   ABEL, J.D., and L.R. THORNTON.   "Responders and Nonresponders to Television Editorials: A Comparison." *Journalism Quarterly* 52 (August 1975):477-84.

788   ADAMS, WILLIAM C. *Television Coverage of International Affairs.* Norwood, N.J.: Ablex, 1982.

789   ADONI, HANNA, AKIBA A. COHEN, and SHERRILL MANE. "Social Reality and Television News: Perceptual Dimensions of Social Conflicts in Selected Life Areas." Journal of Broadcasting 28 (Winter 1984):33-49.

790   ALTER, JONATHAN. "Lessons for the Networks." *Newsweek*, 15 July 1985, 24.
      Analysis of media coverage of international terrorism. Do the networks gullibly fall into the hands of political strategists who use dramatic incidents for publicity? <ED>

791   _____. "The Network Circus: TV Turns up the Emotional Volume." *Newsweek*, 8 July 1985, 21.

792   ALTER, JONATHAN, MICHAEL A. LERNER, and THEODORE STANGER. "Does TV Help Or Hurt?" *Newsweek*, 1 July 1985, 32.

793   ALTHEIDE, DAVID L. *Creating Reality: How Television News Distorts Events*. Beverly Hills, Calif.: Sage, 1974.

Research data based upon interviews, visits to TV stations, and participant organization are synthesized by the author. Pressures to capture ratings, beat deadlines, and avoid scheduling problems combine to encourage superficial coverage of multidimensional stories. Concludes that the main goal of the television newsroom becomes filling each program as easily as possible with *entertaining*, reductive stories. <RR/ED>

794   ____. "Network News: Oversimplified and Underexplained." *Washington Journalism Review*, May 1981, 28-29.

795   ANDERSON, RAYMOND H. "U.S.S.R.: How Lenin's Guidelines Shape the News." Columbia Journalism Review 23 (September/October 1984):40-43.

796   ARIEFF, I. "TV Terrorists: The News Media under Siege." *Videography*, May 1977, 44-46.

797   ATKIN, C.K. "Broadcast News Programming and the Child Audience." *Journal of Broadcasting* 22 (Winter 1978):47-61.

798   BABINGTON, CHARLES. "Helms & Co.: Plotting to Unseat Dan Rather." *Columbia Journalism Review* 24, no. 2 (1985):47.

799   BARRETT, MARVIN, ed. *Broadcast Journalism 1979-1981: The Eighth Alfred I DuPont/Columbia University Survey*. New York: Everest House, 1982.

Three chapters evaluate broadcasters' credibility from the standpoints of (1) their relations with competitors, (2) their coverage of business, and (3) their ability to ferret out and report effectively the *significant* facts behind news stories. Previous reports with these emphases have been printed under various titles. Usually contains at least one article on current legal or ethical dilemma faced by the broadcast journalist. <RR/DM/ED>

800   BASSIOUNI, M. CHERIF. "Media Coverage of Terrorism: The Law and the Public." *Journal of Communication* 32 (Spring 1982):128-43.

801 BEDEL, S. "Is TV Exploiting Tragedy?" *TV Guide*, 16 June 1979, 4-8.

802 BELL, J.B. "Terrorist Scripts and Live Action Spectaculars." *Columbia Journalism Review* 17 (May 1978):47-50.

803 BENNETT, W. LANCE, LYNNE A. GRESSETT, and WILLIAM HALTOM. "Repairing the News: A Case Study of the News Paradigm." *Journal of Communication* 35, no. 2 (1985):50.
      In 1983 a man set fire to himself in Jacksonville, Alabama, as a social statement. For thirty-seven seconds two television camera crewmen recorded the event for a news story without acting to influence the individual or douse the fire. Analysis of ethical implications. <UN/ED>

804 BERGER, ARTHUR ASA, ed. *Television as an Instrument of Terror: Essays on Media Popular and Everyday Life.* New Brunswick, N.J.: Transaction Books, 1979.

805 BROADCASTING. "Calls for a Code on Terrorist Coverage." *Broadcasting,* 22 July 1985, 36.

806 ____. "CBS News' Ground Rules for Terrorist Coverage Backed by Peers, Law Enforcers." *Broadcasting,* 7 November 1977, 42-43.

807 ____. "Closer Look at Network Coverage of TWA Flight 847." *Broadcasting,* 5 August 1985, 58.

808 ____. "Hostage Coverage Hindsight: Competition, Technology Shape the Story. *Broadcasting,* 8 July 1985, 58.

809 BROUSSARD, E., and JACK F. HOLGATE. *Writing and Reporting Broadcast News.* New York: Macmillan, 1982.
      Chapter 13, "Libel, Privacy, Good Taste, and Ethics," includes the texts of the code of broadcast news ethics of the Radio/Television News Directors Association, the Society of Professional Journalists code of ethics, and the National Association of Broadcasters standards of conduct for broadcasting public proceedings. <DLM/ED>

810 BUNNELL, ROBERT, JAMES R. ROSS, KEVIN SETTLAGE, and CHRISTINE TIERNEY. "The Turnstile Journalists: Sawyer, Moyers, Safire & People like Them." *Quill* 70 (July-August 1982):16-21.

This article by American University graduate students examines the ethics of journalists who move in and out of government positions and cover political news during or after their loyalty is established to government employers. <UN/ED>

811   BURKE, CHARLES. "Sleuthing on Local TV: How Much? How Good?" *Columbia Journalism Review* 22 (January-February 1984):43-44.
Undercover reporting by local TV news departments may bring unique advantages, but questions of honesty, privacy, theft, and overzealousness arise. <UN/ED>

812   CASTRO, JANICE. "Smoking Guns, Secret Tapes: A New Skirmish in the War between CBS and Westmoreland." *Time*, 21 May 1984.

813   CATTON, W.R. "Militants and the Media: Partners in Terrorism?" *Indiana Law Journal* 53 (Summer 1978):619-777.
Special Issue: Terrorism and the Media.

814   COOPER, THOMAS W. "Hidden Taping: The Arguments For and the Ethics Against." *Nieman Reports* 42, no. 2 (1987):21-25, 27.
Reviews recent literature justifying the covert taping of news sources by journalists with tape recorders. Author explains nine prominent arguments for and twelve reasons against secret taping. Concludes that source is a person, not a "news object," and must be encountered honestly. <ED>

815   No Entry

816   CRONKITE, WALTER. *The Challenges of Change.* Washington, D.C.: Public Affairs Press, 1971.
A collection of selected speeches by broadcast anchorman Walter Cronkite. Although the topics are wide ranging in scope, many points within several speeches focus upon ethical issues in broadcast journalism. <UN/ED>

817   CRONKITE, WALTER, RICHARD SALANT, and BURTON BENJAMIN. "'News and Views of CBS'.: Walter Cronkite's Reporting Style." *Wall Street Journal,* 21 February 1985, 31, 33.

818   D'AMBROSIO, FREDERICK L. "One from the Heart." *Quill* 75, no. 3 (1987):20-21.

The story of Bud Dwyer committing suicide at a press conference posed problems of decency and sensationalism to editors deciding how to air and print the story. Article is written by executive news producer at WTAE-TV in Pittsburgh, who discusses the decisions he made. <ED>

819   DAVENPORT, LUCINDA D., and RALPH S. IZARD. "Restrictive Policies of the Mass Media." *Journal of Mass Media Ethics* 1, no. 1 (1985):4-9.
    Increasing numbers of news organizations have formal codes of ethics for their personnel. The contents of, values behind, and mechanisms for drafting such codes are discussed. Written codes represented in this survey clearly isolate specific activities and label them as unacceptable or acceptable for journalists. <UN/ED>

820   DIAMOND, EDWIN. "All the News that Isn't News." In *Television and American Culture*. Edited by Carl Lowe. New York: H.W. Wilson Co., 1981.
    A discussion of the nature and characteristics of "hype" in television news. Several examples of its employment and increasing influence are given. <DLM/ED>

821   ____. "Checkbook Journalism Bounces at N.B.C." *Washington Journalism Review* 1 (January-February 1979):32-34.
    Short article on the ethical problems incurred by NBC-TV news in the hiring of two "consultants," former secretary of state Henry Kissinger and former president Gerald Ford. <DLM>

822   ____. "Disco News." *Washington Journalism Review* 1 (September-October 1979):26-28.
    According to this article, news *values* should shape programs. However, "journalists who engage in story from [television] news are unaware of how pervasively certain aesthetic values--for example, consideration of pace, feel and 'look'--shape their work."

823   ____. *Good News, Bad News*. Cambridge: M.I.T. Press, 1978.
    A criticism of the media coverage of the 1976 presidential campaign by an astute political science teacher and journalist/author.

824   DICK, DAVID B. "What Did Mr. Dwyer Do, Daddy?" *Quill* 75, no. 3 (1987):18-20.
    Author argues that television reporters and camera operators were victimized by Budd Dwyer, who committed suicide at a press

conference. He claims that journalists cooperated *unwittingly* before the suicide and *mindlessly* afterward. <TQ/ED>

825 DOMINICK, J.R., ALAN WURTZEL, and GUY LOMETTI. "Television Journalism vs. Show Business: A Content Analysis of Eyewitness News." *Journalism Quarterly* 52 (Summer 1974):213-18.

826 DREW, D.G., and B.B. REEVES. "Children and Television News." *Journalism Quarterly* 57 (Spring 1980):45-54.

827 EFRON, EDITH. *The News Twisters.* Los Angeles: Hash Publishing, 1971.
    Highly critical examination of network television news, which concludes that such news is subjectively and deliberately slanted. Central area of observation is the news *selection* process. Her analytical method to determine bias is the outcome of a grant awarded to evaluate "the tri-network coverage of the then upcoming 1968 presidential campaign." <AU/DLM/ED>

828 EGAN, L.M. "Children's Viewing Patterns for Television News." *Journalism Quarterly* 55 (Summer 1978):337-42.

829 EINSIEDEL, E.F. "Television Network News Coverage of the Eagleton Affair: A Case Study." *Journalism Quarterly* 52 (Spring 1975):56-60.

830 EPSTEIN, EDWARD. *Between Fact and Fiction.* New York: Vintage Books, 1975.
    The last three chapters of this book discuss the ethical problems broadcast journalists face because of competition for ratings, personal biases of reporters, and the ability of the television camera to magnify conflicts. <DLM/ED>

831 ____. *News from Nowhere: Television and the News.* New York: Random House, 1973.
    "Network news is largely, though not entirely, performed and shaped by organizational considerations," according to field study research conducted in the late sixties for a doctoral dissertation. The author concludes that the public must better understand the intrinsic limitations of television. <AU/DLM/ED>

832 ____. "The Uses of 'Terrorism': A Study in Media Bias." *Stanford Journal of International Studies* 12 (1977):67-78.

833   FEDLER, FRED. "Checkbook Journalism Proliferates, Harms Both Public and Media." *Mass Comm Review* 7 (Spring 1980):10-13, 17.

A review of several well-known instances of both broadcast and print organizations paying newsmakers for the privilege of exclusive coverage of a news event. <DLM>

834   FEIGHAN, EDWARD F. "After the Hostage Crisis, TV Focuses on Itself: The Media Debate over Coverage Is Part of the Solution." *New York Times*, 19 August 1985, 19.

835   FERRI, ANTHONY J., and JO E. KELLER. "Perceived Career Barriers for Female Television News Anchors." *Journalism Quarterly* 63, no. 3 (1986):463-67.

836   FRANKEL, ELIOT, and MITCHELL STEPHENS. "All the Obscenity That's Fit to Print." *Washington Journalism Review* 3 (April 1981):15.

An examination by two New York University journalism professors of how broadcast and print media handle obscenity in news reporting. <UN/ED>

837   FULTON, KATHERINE. "Jesse Helms, Journalist." *Columbia Journalism Review* 24, no. 2 (1985):50.

838   GALICIAN, MARY LOU. "Perceptions of Good News and Bad News on Television." *Journalism Quarterly* 63, no. 3 (1986):611-15.

839   GAMSON, WILLIAM A. *What's News: A Game Simulation of TV News.* New York: Free Press, 1984.

One chapter acquaints the students with several types of pressure exerted on the television newsroom. These call for ethical decisions if one wants to play the "game." As a game simulation, the book invites readers to play the roles of newsroom professionals. <DLM/ED>

840   GANS, H.J. *Deciding What's News: A Study of CBS News, NBC Nightly News, Newsweek, and Time.* New York: Pantheon Books, 1979.

Sociological study divided into three parts: (1) the news itself and underlying values, (2) the journalists and their sources, objectivity, and values, and (3) news policy. The norms of "CBS Evening News," "NBC Nightly News," *Newsweek,* and *Time,* and decision-making

126

processes regarding the content of news products, are closely inspected. <DLM/ED>

841   GHAREEB, EDMUND, ed. *Split Vision: The Portrayal of Arabs in the American Media.* Washington, D.C.: American-Arab Affairs Council, 1983.

842   GIRARD, TOM. "Not in the Murrow Tradition: the '60 Minutes' Libel Case." *Variety,* 15 June 1983, 39.

843   GLASSER, THEODORE L. "On the Morality of Secretly Taped Interviews." *Neiman Reports* 39 (Spring 1985): 17-20.
      Through logic, quotation of philosophical authority, and reasoned refutation, author challenges the most common arguments against the secret taping of news sources by reporters (for example, taping does not invade privacy: it is not the same as entrapment or eavesdropping). <ED>

844   GOLDMAN, KEVIN. "Is NBC Over-Marketing Brokaw?" *Variety,* 25 December 1985, 32.

845   GOODWIN, H. EUGENE. "News Media Ethics--Where Should It Be Taught and By Whom?" *Mass Comm Review* 8, no.2 (1981):11-16.

846   GORDAN, JIM. "A Question of Ethics." *News Photographer,* July 1983, 11-19.
      Analyzes the ethical implications of an incident in which television news photographer filmed a despondent man who publicly set fire to himself. The photographer filmed almost two minutes before attempting to aid the man. Includes selected responses to the incident from journalists, editors, and academics. <RR/ED>

847   HEUMANN, JOE. "U.S. Network Television: Melodrama and the Iranian Crisis." *Middle East Review* 12 (Summer-Fall 1980):51-55.

848   HICKEY, N. "Terrorism and Television." Part 1. *TV Guide,* 31 July 1976, 2-6.

849   ____. "Terrorism and Television." Part 2. *TV Guide,* 7 August 1976, 10-13.

850 HICKEY, NEIL. "Was the Truth Buried at Wounded Knee?" *TV Guide,* 1,8,15, and 22 December 1973.

851 HILL, FREDERIC B. "Media Diplomacy: Crisis Management with an Eye on the TV Screen." *Washington Journalism Review,* May 1981, 23-27.

852 HOFSTETTER, C. RICHARD. *Bias in the News.* Columbus: Ohio State University Press, 1976.
    Content analysis of 4,349 network television news stories on the 1972 presidential election campaign. Concludes that coverage by ABC, CBS, and NBC was not politically biased. Coverage did vary, however, in amount of time devoted to candidates, in how reports were augmented by actualities, and in the placement of coverage within the broadcast half-hours. Chapter 1 usefully separates bias into three types: lying, distortion, and value assertion. <RR/DLM/ED>

853 HOHENBERG, JOHN. *The News Media; A Journalist Looks at His Profession.* New York: Holt, Rinehart, and Winston, 1968.
    The final chapter in part 1 criticizes television news for paltry public affairs coverage and obsession with gimmicks to improve ratings. Part 2 contains ten chapters that consider specific ethical issues including lack of credibility, pack journalism, press junkets, and the increasing ration of soft feature stories to hard news. <RR/ED>

854 IGNATIEFF, MICHAEL. "TV and the Ethics of Victimhood." *Harpers,* February 1986, 14.

855 ITULE, BRUCE D., and DOUGLAS A. ANDERSON. *News Writing and Reporting for Today's Media.* New York: Random House, 1987.
    Although primarily a how-to textbook for future reporters and newswriters, the chapters entitled "Ethics: Responsibility to Society" and "Law" are useful introductions for the future professional. <ED>

856 JOHNSON, KIRK A. "Black and White in Boston." *Columbia Journalism Review* 26, no. 1 (May-June 1987):50-54.
    A Study financed by the Trotter Institute of the University of Massachusetts, Boston, showed major biases in mainstream coverage of blacks within a sample of 3,200 news stories. Author chose six of the largest metropolitan news outlets including WBZ-TV, WCVB-TV, and WGBH-TV. <ED>

857   JONES, ALEX S.   "TV in the Hostage Crises: Reporter or Participant?" *New York Times,* 2 July 1985, 1.
      Concerns the Beirut hostage crises.

858   KAISER, CHARLES.   "Newsmen and Their Perks." *Newsweek,* 9 May 1983, 44.
      A one-page article on journalists accepting gifts from outside organizations, in which motivations of gift-givers are unclear and in which public perception of the media may damage journalistic credibility. Examples from broadcast media. <DLM/ED>

859   KATZ, LEE MICHAEL.   "Our Job Is to Engage Viewer, Not Distract." *USA Today,* 23 April 1984, 11-A.
      Transcript of Tom Brokaw interview about his role as "NBC Nightly News" anchorman. Brokaw discusses election day exit polling and television camera crews "badgering" public figures at the newsmakers' homes. <DLM>

860   LAPHAM, LEWIS H.   "Gilding the News." *Harper's,* July 1981, 31-39.

861   LEFEVER, ERNEST W.   "News and Views at CBS." *Wall Street Journal,* 18 April 1985.

862   LEROY, DAVID J., and CHRISTOPHER H. STERLING.   *Mass News: Practices, Controversies, and Alternatives.* Englewood Cliffs, N.J.: Prentice-Hall, 1973.
      Heavily weighted toward television, this collection of twenty-six articles is divided into four sections: (1) context of mass news, (2) practice of mass news, (3) alternatives in mass news, and (4) controversies in mass news. <RR/DLM/ED>

863   LEVINE, GRACE FERRARI.   "'Learned Helplessness' and the Evening News." *Journal of Communication* 27 (Fall 1977):100-5.

864   _____.   "Learned Helplessness in Local TV News." *Journalism Quarterly* 63, no. 1 (1986):12-18.

865   LOFTUS, JACK.   "Are TV Webs Hostage in Beirut?   No, Say Broadcasters: Praise Coverage." *Variety,* 26 June 1985, 1.

866   LOWRY, D.T. "Measures of Network News Bias in the 1972 Presidential Campaign." *Journal of Broadcasting* 18 (Fall 1974):387-402.

867   MC BRIDE, DONALD L. *Resources for Teaching about Journalism Ethics: An Annotated Bibliography.* Project of the Professional Freedom and Responsibility Committee, Radio and Television Journalism Division, Association for Education in Journalism and Mass Communication, 1984.
      A bibliography listing sixty-three significant texts and articles, many of which are included in this bibliography. Available from Donald L. McBride, Department of Journalism and Mass Communication, South Dakota State University, Brookings, S.D. 57007. <DLM/ED>

868   MC CAIN, T.A. "Effect of Camera Angle on Source Credibility Attraction." *Journal of Broadcasting* 21 (Winter 1977):35-46.

869   MADDEN, PAUL. "Banned, Censored and Delayed: A Chronology of Some TV Programs Dealing with Northern Ireland." In *The British Media and Ireland.* London: Campaign for Free Speech in Ireland, 1978.

870   MADLIN, N. "ABC's Eyewitness Anonymous." *Columbia Journalism Review* 22 (July-August 1983):32-33.

871   MANDELBAUM, M. "Vietnam: The Television War." *Daedalus* 111 (Fall 1982):157-69.

872   MARKS, JEFFREY. "The Dwyer Story Will Happen Again in a Different Form." *RTNDA Communicator* 41, no. 3 (1987):31-32.
      Includes quotes and analysis of news directors who elected to broadcast or not to broadcast the Budd Dwyer suicide at a Harrisburg, Pa., news conference. The author, chairman of the Radio-Television News Directors Association's Ethics and Standards Committee, considers germane policy implications for newsrooms. <ED>

873   MATUSOW, BARBARA. *The Evening Stars.* Boston: Houghton Mifflin, 1983.
      An examination of the financial pressures upon U.S. television news professionals deriving from competition for ratings. "For every dollar spent gathering the news, two dollars are spent on 'cosmetics'--

expensive sets, promotional campaigns, grossly inflated anchor salaries, helicopters, and other gimmicks." <DLM/ED>

874　MAUSHART, S. "See Jane Watch; Watch Jane Watch: Students Discuss TV News." *Etc.* 38 (Fall 1983):285-89.

875　MEESKE, MILAN D., and MOHAMAD HAMID JAVAHERI. "Network Television Coverage of the Iranian Hostage Crisis." *Journalism Quarterly* 59 (Winter 1982):641-45.

876　MENCHER, MELVIN. *News Reporting and Writing.* Dubuque, Iowa: W.C. Brown, 1984.
　　　Section 5, on risks and responsibilities, includes chapters on the law, taste, and morality of journalism, particularly as relevant to reports. <RR/ED>

877　MICHIE, LARRY. "Marketing Virus Infecting TV News." *Variety,* 14 May 1986, 50.

878　MILLER, MARK. "How TV Covers War." *New Republic* 187 (November 1982):26-33.
　　　The claim is often advanced that the television camera is an unbiased instrument. The author claims that this assumption could lead to the opposite possibility, that television is the *most* biased of the media because its visual bias is least detected and conceals or distracts from other forms of bias. <DLM/ED>

879　MITCHELL, GAYLE, and DOUG BATES. "The Toughest Call." *Quill* 75, no. 4 (1987):27-29.
　　　Discusses story of mother and three children who were shot near Eugene, Oregon, and the related follow-up stories. Since the mother herself was eventually revealed as the perpetrator of the shootings, questions of media gullibility and responsibility to follow-up are considered. Comparative approaches of a local television station and a newspaper. <ED>

880　NEWMAN, JAY B. "The Dwyer Suicide: Should Pictures Be Shown?" *RTNDA Communicator,* March 1987, 30.
　　　News director at WCAU-TV in Philadelphia describes factors weighed by professional broadcast journalist prior to editing images of Budd Dwyer, who committed suicide at a press conference in Harrisburg, Pa. <ED>

881   NIMMO, DAN. *Newsgathering in Washington: A Study in Political Communication*. New York: Atherton Press, 1964.

882   NORTHRIP, CHARLES M. "A Study of the Ethics Criteria Used by Television Newsmen in Florida." M.A. Thesis, University of Florida, 1963.
       One of the early studies of broadcast journalism ethics. Although the categories are useful for other studies, the data are over twenty-five years old, are limited to a single state, and were assembled as a master's thesis when few previous or similar studies could be compared. <DLM/ED>

883   PICARD, ROBERT G. "The Conundrum of News Coverage of Terrorism." Speech presented to the International Terrorism and Human Rights Symposium of the Toledo International Law Society, University of Toledo, 8 February 1987.

884   _____. "Words on War and Conflict." *St. Louis Journalism Review*, September 1983, 21-22.

885   PIERCE, J.C. "Party, Ideology, and Public Evaluations of the Power of Television Newspeople." *Journalism Quarterly* 54 (Summer 1977):307-12.

886   POLSKIN, HOWARD. "Reporter's Dilemma: Save a Life or Get the Story?" *TV Guide* 23 July 1983, 4-8.
       Describes incident in which newsmen filmed a despondent man immolating himself. Considers the degree to which journalists should become involved in news stories. <RR/ED>

887   POWELL, JODY. "Rating the Press: Reporting Hostage Crises." *Los Angeles Times* 30 June 1985, 5.

888   POWERS, RON. *The Newscasters*. New York: St. Martin's Press, 1977.

889   RASKY, SUSAN F. "Terror Coverage on TV Is Criticized: But House Panel Is Told that Highjacking Should Not Lead to Industry-Wide Rules." *New York Times* 31 July 1985, 3.

890   RITCHIE, DANIEL. "Broadcast News Is Trusted, but We Must Be Sensitive to Our Tremendous Power." *Television/Radio Age*, 20 August 1984, 45.

891 ROBERTS, C. "Presentation of Blacks in Television Network Newscasts." *Journalism Quarterly* 52 (Spring 1975):50-55.

892 ROBINSON, M.J., and K.A. MC PHERSON. "Television News Coverage Before the 1976 New Hampshire Primary: The Focus of Network Journalism." *Journal of Broadcasting* 21 (Spring 1977):177-86.

893 ROSENSTIEL, THOMAS B. "Murrow Docudrama Splits Journalists: Time Inc. Accused of Using Reporters' Group to Push File." *Los Angeles Times*, 7 December 1985, 28.

894 SALHOLZ, ELOISE, STILLE, ALEXANDER, and MORRIS, HOLLY. "Turning an Eye on the Lurid." *Newsweek*, 7 May 1984, 83.
     A half-page discussion of the ethics of the cable news network in providing live coverage of trials of alleged rapists and child sex molesters. <DLM/ED>

895 SALTZMAN, JOE. "Television Interviewing Techniques: Ramifications of Westmoreland vs. CBS." *USA Today*, September 1985, 85.

896 SCHLESINGER, PHILIP, GRAHAM MURDOCK, and PHILIP ELLIOTT. *Televising 'Terrorism': Political Violence in Popular Culture*. London: Comedia, 1983.

897 SHOOK, FREDERICK. *The Process of Electronic News Gathering*. Englewood, Co.: Morton, 1982.
     One chapter about the ethics of ENG reporting highlights the ethical problems of immediacy in news broadcasts. <DLM/ED>

898 SHOOK, FREDERICK, and DAN LATTIMORE. *The Broadcast News Process*. Englewood, Co.: Morton, 1982.
     Part 4 of this college text concerns the regulation and ethics of broadcast journalism. Chapters on "Legal Considerations," "Ratings Versus Professionalism," and "Broadcast Editorials" conclude with exercises for students. Several appendices include journalism codes of ethics. <DLM/ED>

899 SMEYAK, PAUL G. *Broadcast News Writing*. 2d ed. New York: Macmillan, 1983.

Although the book primarily introduces students to broadcast newswriting fundamentals, appendices include the Radio/Television News Directors Association code of broadcast news ethics, the Television Code (Published by the Code authority of the National Association of Broadcasters), and a statement of principles of the bench, bar, and press of the state of Kansas. <KS/ED>

900   SMITH, C. FRASER. "Reporting Grief: Marine Families Review the Press Invasion." *Washington Journalism Review*, March 1984, 21-22+.

901   STEPHENS, MITCHELL. *Broadcast News*. New York: Rinehart & Wilson, 1980.
      This college-level test includes an almost comprehensive chapter on broadcast news ethics and law. Issues include conflict on interest, privacy, disorder, panic, staging, hidden microphones, and protection of sources. <DLM/ED>

902   SULLIVAN, JAMES MICHAEL. "TV Newsmen--Stop Cheating My Children." *Intellect* 106, no. 2395 (1978):393-94. [ERIC: EJ182845].
      Examines the dangers and disappointments of television journalism. Focuses upon core issues that demonstrate the factors that keep TV news from becoming the positive social force it has the potential to become. <AU/RK/ED>

903   SURFACE, BILL. "Should Reporters Buy News?" *Saturday Review* 50, no. 19 (13 May 1967):85-86.
      When broadcast and print journalists are offered news for a fee, several ethical issues must be carefully considered. <DLM/ED>

904   TELEVISION/RADIO AGE. "Many Stations Enact Guidelines on Involvement with Terrorists." *Television/Radio Age*. 24 October 1977.

905   TERRY, H.A. "Television and Terrorism: Professionalism Not Quite the Answer." *Indiana Law Journal* 53 (Summer 1978):619-777.
      Special issue: Terrorism and the media.

906   TUCHMAN, GAYE. *Making News: A Study in the Construction of Reality*. New York: Free Press, 1978.
      Principal thesis is that news is a socially constructed product, built by professionals as a matter of working routine. News, it is

argued, is determined through negotiations between source and reporter, between reporter and editor. The news presented to the public largely legitimates the status quo. Based upon ten years of field work in East Coast newspaper and television newsrooms. <RR/ED>

907 TURK, JUDY VANSLYKE. "Information Subsidies and Media Content: A Study of Public Relations Influence on the News." *Journalism Monographs*. 100 (December 1986):1-29.

908 VARIETY. "Buchwald Assails TV News Anchors during Coast Fete." *Variety*, 23 October 1985, 22.

909 WALZER, MICHAEL. "Follow That Network: NBC Interview with Abu Abbas." *New Republic* 194 (2 June 1986): 8.

910 WATSON, GEORGE. "Turning TV over to the Audience." *Broadcasting*, 9 July 1984, 22.
   This one-page commentary by the vice president of ABC news concerns "Viewpoint," the ABC network television program that presents ethical issues in broadcast journalism. Watson asserts that despite occasional ethical problems within U.S. Television practices, American audiences are nevertheless highly supportive of the journalistic methods of U.S. television networks. <DLM/ED>

911 WEAVER, PAUL H. "Is Television News Biased?" *Public Interest* 26 (Winter 1972):57-74.
   Concludes that television news is biased: "A more useful question to pose is: *Which* biases are we content to let journalism possess, and which do we insist that it avoid?" Includes review of Edith Efron's book *The News Twisters* (see entry 827). <DLM/ED>

912 WEINRAUB, BERNARD. "ABC News Said It Erred in Airing Unchallenged Views of a Russian: Vladmir Posner's Comments on Ronald Reagan's Speech on Military Spending." *New York Times*, 28 February 1986, 1, 4.

913 WEISMAN, J. "When Hostages' Lives Are at Stake, Should a TV Reporter Push on or Pull Back?" *TV Guide*, 26 August 1978, 4-9.

914 WENGLENSKY, M. "Television News: A New Slant." *Columbia Forum* 3 (Fall 1979):2-9.

915 WICKER, TOM. "Not a Pseudo-Event." *New York Times*, 9 July 1985, 27.

Wicker's column concerns television and the TWA hijacking incident.

916 WILBER, HAROLD B. "Role of the Media during a Terrorist Incident." *FBI Law Enforcement Bulletin* 54, no. 4 (1985):20-23.

917 WILL, GEORGE F. "A Journalist Is a Citizen Also." *ASNE Bulletin*, November 1983, 12-13.

The TV commentator and newspaper columnist defends his part in helping to coach Ronald Reagan before the 1980 presidential debates. Accompanying articles by Hugh Sidey and Alexander C. Hutchison debate the pros and cons of Will's actions. <UN/ED>

918 WILSON, D. "News from Nowhere." *Sight & Sound* 44 (Winter 1974):45-48.

919 WULFEMEYER, TIM K., and LORI L. MCFADDEN. "Anonymous Attribution in Network News." *Journalism Quarterly* 63, no. 3 (1986):468-73.

920 WURTH-HOUGH, SANDRA. "Network News Coverage of Terrorism: The Early Years." *Terrorism* 6 (1983):403-22.

II F. TELEVISION, POLITICS, AND GOVERNMENT

921   ANSON, ROBERT SAM. "The World According to Garth." *New Times*, 30 October 1978.

    After sixty-seven wins and sixteen defeats, David Garth was heavyweight champion of American television politics when this article was written. Describes Garth's strategy, attitude, campaigns, life-style, and media philosophy. Implicit ethical questions about the profession and practice of converting a multidimensional human being into a two-dimensional thirty-second commercial that reduces political issues to slogans and jingles. <ED>

922   ATWOOD, L.E., and K.R. SANDERS. "Perception of Information Sources and the Likelihood of Split Ticket Voting." *Journalism Quarterly* 52 (August 1975):421-28.

923   BABINGTON, CHARLES. "Helms & Co.: Plotting to Unseat Dan Rather." *Columbia Journalism Review* 24, no. 2 (1985):47.

924   BALON, R.E. "Candidate Image in a Broadcast Debate." *Journal of Broadcasting* 19 (Spring 1975):181-93.

925   BARKIN, S.M.   "Eisenhower's Television Planning Board: An Unwritten Chapter in the History of Political Broadcasting." *Journal of Broadcasting* 27 (Fall 1983):319-31.

926   BARKIN, S.M., and MICHAEL GUREVITCH. "Out of Work and on the Air: Television News of Unemployment." *Critical Studies in Mass Communication* 4, no. 1 (1987):2-19.
        Assuming the inherently political nature of television content and the broadcasting industry, the authors examine television news coverage of unemployment during the first six months of 1983. Questions are raised about whether television acts as a disseminator of a "dominant ideology" or as a "cultural forum." <ED>

927   BARRETT, MARVIN, ed. *Broadcast Journalism, 1979-81.* New York: Everest House, 1982.
        Features articles on the political coverage of 1980 presidential elections.   Other subjects include public affairs broadcasting, responsibilities of the broadcast journalist, and credibility. Compendium is the eighth Alfred I. DuPont Columbia University survey.

928   BECKTOLT, WARREN, JR., JOSEPH HILYARD, and CARL R. BYBEE.   "Agenda Control in the 1976 Debates: A Content Analysis." *Journalism Quarterly* 54 (Winter 1977):674-81.

929   BENSON, THOMAS W.   "Another Shooting in Cowtown." *Quarterly Journal of Speech* 67, no. 4 (1981):347-406.
        The production of a series of political television commercials for a congressional candidate in the Southwest in 1979 is scrutinized. A teacher of political communication courses participated in the commercial production and then wrote this article. <PD/ED>

930   BLANKENBURG, W.G.   "Nixon vs. the Networks: Madison Avenue and Wall Street." *Journal of Broadcasting* 21 (Spring 1977):163-75.

931   BLANKENSHIP, JANE, MARLENE G. FINE, and LESLIE K. DAVIS. "1980 Republican Primary Debates: The Transformation of Actor to Scene." *Quarterly Journal of Speech* 69 (February 1983):25-36.

932   BROWN, JAMES. "Reporting the Vote on Election Night." *Journal of Communication* 28 (Fall 1978):132-38.

933 BUNNELL, ROBERT, JAMES R. ROSS, KEVIN SETTLAGE, and CHRISTINE TIERNEY. "The Turnstile Journalists: Sawyer, Moyers, Safire and People Like Them." *Quill,* July-August 1982, 16-21.

What are the ethical decisions faced by journalists who take, and later return to journalism from, government positions? Four American University graduate students examine this question and consider specific cases. <UN/ED>

934 CANDEE, DAN. "The Moral Psychology of Watergate." *Journal of Social Issues* 31, no. 2 (1975):183-92.

935 CHESLER, EDWARD W. *Radio, Television and American Politics.* New York: Sheed & Ward, 1969.

936 CHRISTIANS, CLIFFORD. "The 1976 Campaign and TV Advertising." *Illinois Business Review* 33, no. 5 (1976):6-8.

937 CUTBIRTH, CRAG W., M.E. SHAPIRO, and W. WILLIAMS. "The Ethics of Media Framing of Issues in the 1980 Presidential Campaign." Paper presented at the annual meeting of the International Communication Association, Dallas, Texas, 26-30 May 1983. [ERIC: ED233412]

A study examined 158 economy-related news stories broadcast by ABC-TV, NBC-TV, and CBS- TV during the fall of 1980. Analysis considered whether the economic reports supported or denigrated specific candidates. The researchers concluded that ABC and NBC each committed four ethical violations, and CBS committed two. <MM/ED>

938 DESMOND, R.J., and T.R. DONAHUE. "Role of the 1976 Televised Presidential Debates in the Political Socialization of Adolescents." *Communication Quarterly* 29 (Fall 1981):302-8.

939 DIAMOND, EDWIN. "Checkbook Journalism Bounces at N.B.C." *Washington Journalism Review* 1 (January-February 1979):32-34.

A brief article on the ethical problems incurred by NBC-TV news when the network hired "consultants" with top-flight firsthand experience. Former president Gerald Ford and former secretary of state Henry Kissinger may have been motivated because of their previous positions by partisan vision and a lack of journalistic skepticism toward political authority. <DLM/ED>

940 ____. *Good News, Bad News.* Cambridge: M.I.T. Press, 1978.
      In-depth criticism of the media coverage of the 1976 U.S. presidential campaign.

941 DONALDSON, SAM. "Bulldogging Presidents." *Quill* 75, no. 5 (1987):18-23.
      Outspoken network White House correspondent defends the role of an inquisitive, aggressive presidential press corps. Argues that it is not privacy that is invaded but rather the public who is protected when the president is cross-examined and constantly probed. <ED>

942 DORFMAN, RON. "Peeping Watchdogs." *Quill* 75, no. 6 (1987):15-16.
      Covers the pros and cons not only of the Gary Hart-Donna Rice coverage but also of the history of "candidate smothering" by the press. Emphasizes Hart's knowledge of the Eagleton exposé and his awareness that the Rice rendezvous might well receive similar treatment.

943 EINSEIDEL, E.F. "Television Network News Coverage of the Eagleton Affair: A Case Study." *Journalism Quarterly* 52 (Spring 1975):56-60.

944 EVARTS, G., and G.H. STEMPEL. "Coverage of the 1972 Campaign by TV, News Magazines, and Major Newspapers." *Journalism Quarterly* 51 (Winter 1974):645-48.

945 FESTA, REGINA, and LUIZ SANTORO. "Policies from Below--Alternative Video in Brazil." *Media Development* 34, no. 1 (1987):27-29
      Demonstrates that government policies and regulations need not be monolithic. Shows that video may be distributed and regulated by policy "from below" by grass-roots distributors and producers with minimal exposure to the censorship and bureaucracies of government--in this case, in Brazil. <ED>

946 FLETCHER, JOSEPH FRANCIS. "Commercial versus Public Television Audiences: Public Activities and the Watergate Hearings." *Communication Quarterly* 25 (Fall 1977):13-16.

947 FRENCH, IRENE. "TV Host Gets Axe after Hatchet Job on the Governor." *Variety*, 16 December 1981, 33.

948   FROMM, JOSEPH. "TV: Does It Box in the President in a Crisis?" *U.S. News and World Report*, 15 July 1985, 23.

949   FULTON, KATHERINE. "Jesse Helms, Journalist." *Columbia Journalism Review* 24, no. 2 (1985):50.

950   GILBERT, ROBERT E. *Television and Presidential Politics.* North Quincy, Mass.: Christopher Publishing House, 1972.

951   GIRARD, TOM.   "Sauter Scolds Press Critics of Nixon Deal (Purchase of Pretaped Interviews by CBS). *Variety,* 28 March 1974, 48.

952   HALEY, W. "Politics in the Television Age." *Times Literary Supplement* (London), no. 3914, March 1977, 286-88.

953   HALLIN, DANIEL C. *"The Uncensored War":   The Media and Vietnam.* Newbury Park, Calif.: Sage, 1986.

954   HARRISON, JOHN M. "Media, Men, and Morality." *Review of Politics* 36, no. 2 (1974):250-55.

955   HOWARD, A. "Parties, Elections, and Television." *Sight & Sound* 47 (August 1978):206-9.

956   IRVING, KRISTOL. "Creative Coverage of Political News." *Wall Street Journal,* 11 October 1984, 30, 32.

957   JACKSON-BEECK, MARILYN, and ROBERT G. MEADOW. "The Triple Agenda of Presidential Debates." *Public Opinion Quarterly* 43, no. 2 (1979):173-80.
       Little support is found for the view that televised presidential debates address the public's primary political concerns. Based upon (1) content analysis of the first 1960 and 1976 presidential debates and (2) secondary analysis of survey data (Gallup and Center for Political Studies). Candidates, journalists, and public appear to have separate agenda issues. The function, format, and value, if any, of debates should also be debated. < UN/ED >

958   JAMIESON, KATHLEEN HALL. *Packaging the Presidency: A History and Criticism of Presidential Campaign Advertising.* Newbury Park, Calif.: Sage, 1984.

959   JOHNSON, N. "The Politics of Television and the Television of Politics: Three Views." *Quarterly Review of Film Studies* 8 (Fall 1983):39-43.

960   JOSLYN, R.A. "Content of Political Spot Ads." *Journalism Quarterly* 57 (Spring 1980):92-98.

961   JUDIS, JOHN B. "The Hart Affair." *Columbia Journalism Review* 26, no. 2 (July-August 1987):21-25.
        Analysis of coverage, particularly by the *Miami Herald* and other U.S. Newspapers, of Gary Hart's relationship with model Donna Rice. Claims that both Hart and the press had weaknesses: while Hart was living a life "he could not justify or reveal," the press was guilty of "unwonted recklessness," "sensationalism and scandal-mongering." The concrete examples listed did pertain to print journalism, but the author aims his commentary at journalism as a profession. <ED>

962   KEPPLINGER, HANS. "Visual Biases in Television Campaign Coverage." *Communication Research* 9, no. 3 (1982):432-46.
        A West German study of how bias enters the shooting and editing of visual material, particularly in the coverage of political campaigns. <DLM/ED>

963   LANG, KURT, and GLADYS LANG. *Politics and Television.* Chicago: Quadrangle Books, 1968.

964   LERNER, MAX A. "A Billion Dollar Election." *Newsweek,* 8 November 1982, 32.

965   LEROY, DAVID J., and LESLIE F. SMITH. "Perceived Ethicality of Some TV News Production Techniques by a sample of Florida Legislators." *Speech Monographs* 40, no. 4 (1973): 326-29.
        Pilot study of ethical attitudes of politicians toward TV production techniques in news coverage. The primary influential factor in judging ethicality seemed to be editorial intention; where the intention appeared to be deceitful, unethicality was perceived. <UN/ED>

966   LINSKY, MARTIN. *Impact: How the Press Affects Federal Policymaking.* New York: W.W. Norton, 1986.

967   ____. "Is a Straw Poll Worth Reporting?" *The Hastings Center Report* (Hastings-on-Hudson, N.Y.), June 1983, 12-13.

968 LINSKY, MARTIN, JONATHAN MOORE, WENDY O'DONNELL, and DAVID WHITMAN. *How the Press Affects Federal Policymaking: Six Case Studies*. New York: W.W. Norton, 1986.

969 LOWRY, D.T. "Measures of Network News Bias in the 1972 Presidential Campaign." *Journal of Broadcasting* 18 (Fall 1974):387-402.

970 MC CARTHY, EUGENE. "Sins of Omission: The Media as Censor." *Harper's*, June 1977, 90-92.

971 MC LEOD, JACK M., CARL R. BYBEE, and JEAN A. DORALL. "The 1976 Presidential Debates and the Equivalence of Informed Political Participation." Paper presented at a meeting of the International Communication Association, Chicago, Illinois, 1978. [ERIC: ED155121]
    Television news viewing and campaign advertising recall had weaker effects than newspaper reading, according to this 1978 investigation of the 1976 presidential debates. <AU/AV/ED>

972 MENDELSON, HAROLD, and IRVING CRESPI. *Polls, Television, and the New Politics*. Scranton, Pa.: Chandler Publishing, 1970.

973 MICKELSON, SIGMOND. *The Electronic Mirror: Politics in the Age of Television*. New York: Dodd, Mead, 1972.

974 MINOW, NEWTON N., JOHN BARTLOW MARTIN, and LEE M. MITCHELL. *Presidential Television*. New York: Basic Books, 1973.

975 NIMMO, DAN. *Newsgathering in Washington: A Study in Political Communication*. New York: Atherton Press, 1964.

976 ____. *The Political Persuaders: The Techniques of Modern Election Campaigns*. Englewood Cliffs, N.J.: Prentice-Hall, 1970.

977 NIMMO, DAN, and JAMES E. COMBS. *Mediated Political Realities*. New York: Longman, 1983.

978 NORDENSTRENG, KAARLE. *The Mass Media Declaration of UNESCO.* Norwood, N.J.: Ablex, 1984.

979 O'KEEFE, G.J. "Political Malaise and Reliance on Media." *Journalism Quarterly* 57 (Spring 1980):122-28.

980 OSTROFF, D.H. "Participant-Observer Study of TV Campaign Coverage." *Journalism Quarterly* 57 (Spring 1980):415-19.

981 OVERLAND, D. "Great Watergate Conspiracy! A TV Blitzkrieg?" *Contemporary Rhetoric* 233 (July 1978):29-32.

982 PARANTI, MICHAEL. *Inventing Reality.* New York: St. Martin's, 1986.

983 PEPPER, ROBERT. "Election Night 1972: TV Network Coverage." *Journal of Broadcasting* 18 (Winter 1973-74):27-38.

984 PIERCE, J.C. "Party, Ideology, and Public Evaluations of the Power of Television Newspeople." *Journalism Quarterly* 54 (Summer 1977):307-12.

985 PIPPERT, WESLEY. "Morality and Communications: The Presidency." *Vital Speeches,* April 1983, 379.

986 PRISUTA, ROBERT H. "Televised Sports and Political Values." *Journal of Communication* 29, no. 1 (1979):94-102.
     The general premise that levels of conservative political values in adolescents are related to exposure to and involvement in televised sports was tested. Some of the values with which the correlation occurs are authoritarianism, nationalism, need-determined expression, and general conservatism. General television viewing is also a strong predictor of conservatism. Three tables. <UN/ED>

987 RITCHIE, DANIEL L. "Local TV Stations Should Be Channels for Network Reform." *Minneapolis Star and Tribune,* 17 April 1984, 11-A.
     A quarter-page commentary opposing the broadcast of exit-poll data until all polls are closed on election day as perceived by the chairman and chief executive officer of Group W. <DLM/ED>

988 ROBINSON, M.J., and K.A. MC PHERSON. "Television News Coverage before the 1976 New Hampshire Primary: The Focus of

Network Journalism." *Journal of Broadcasting* 21 (Spring 1977):177-86.

989   RUBIN, A.M. "Child and Adolescent Television Use and Political Socialization." *Journalism Quarterly* 55 (Spring 1978):125-29.

990   SANDELL, K.L., and D.H. OSTROFF. "Political Information Content and Children's Political Socialization." *Journal of Broadcasting* 25 (Winter 1981):49-59.

991   SHYLES, L.C. "Defining the Issues of a Presidential Election from Televised Political Spot Advertisements." *Journal of Broadcasting* 27 (Fall 1983):333-43.

992   THOMAS, PAMELA. "Policies and Politics: Television and Video in the South Pacific." *Media Development* 34, no. 1 (1987):17-19.
      Author notes the absence of and need for government policies regulating use of video and television throughout Pacific island societies. Describes the "inverse" (video preceded broadcast television) visual electronic revolution of the South Pacific and the one-sided control U.S. and Australian multimedia corporations will have over island programming. <ED>

993   WHALE, JOHN. *The Half-Shut Eye: Television and Politics in Britain and America.* New York: St. Martin's, 1969.

994   WILHELMSON, FREDERICK D., and JANE BRET. *Telepolitics: The Politics of Neuronic Man.* Plattsburgh, N.Y.: Tundra Books, 1972.

995   WISE, DAVID. *Politics of Lying: Government Deception, Secrey, and Power.* New York: Random House, 1973.

996   WOMACK, D., and J.R. HOAR. "Treatment of Candidates in Convention Floor Interviews." *Journalism Quarterly* 58 (Summer 1981):300-2.

997   WORTON, STANLEY N. *Freedom of Speech and Press.* Rochelle Park, N.J.: Hayden Book Co., 1975.

II G. ETHICS AND TELEVISION'S EFFECTS

998   ATKIN, CHARLES. "Effects of Realistic TV Violence vs. Fictional Violence on Aggression." *Journalism Quarterly* 60 (Winter 1983):615-21.

999   ____. "Political Advertising Effects on Voters and Children." Paper presented at the annual meeting of the American Psychological Association, Washington, D.C., 3-7 September 1976. [ERIC: ED147200]

1000 ATKIN, CHARLES, B.S. GREENBERG, and S. MC DERMOTT. "Television and Race Role Socialization." *Journalism Quarterly* 60 (August 1983):407-14.
        Effects of political television commercials upon voting behavior are examined. The role of voter-oriented ads in the socializing of children to the political environment is inspected. Conclusions include findings that advertising aimed at adult voters may contribute to socializing children toward a political outlook. <AU/DB/ED>

1001 ATKIN, CHARLES, JOHN P. MURRAY, and OGUZ P. NAYMAN. "The Surgeon General's Research Program on

Television and Social Behavior: A Review of Empirical Findings."
Journal of Broadcasting 17 (Winter 1973):21-35.

1002   BALON, R.E. "Impact of 'Roots' on a Racially Heterogeneous
        Southern Community: An Exploratory Study." *Journalism of
        Broadcasting* 22 (Summer 1978):299-307.

1003   BARAN, STANLEY. "TV Programming and Attitudes toward
        Mental Retardation." *Journalism Quarterly* 54 (Spring 1977):140-42.

1004   BIZZELL, PATRICIA L. "The Ethos of Academic Discourse."
        College Composition and Communication. 29, no. 4 (1978):351-55.
        Effects of television viewing upon students' abilities to conduct
rational arguments. Suggests students should be encouraged to provide
proof in their writing. <DD/ED>

1005   BLANK, DAVID M. "Final Comments on the Violence Profile."
        Journal of Broadcasting 21 (Summer 1977):287-96.

1006   _____. "The Gerbner Violence Profile." *Journal of Broadcasting* 21
        (Summer 1977):273-79.

1007   COELHO, GEORGE V., ed. *Television as a Teacher: A Research
        Monograph.* Bethesda, Md.: National Institute of Mental Health
        (DHHS), 1981. [ERIC: ED225549].
        Ten social researchers and mental health specialists review and
compress significant areas of expertise to assess the role of television as
a teacher influencing mental health and attitudes. Collection of papers.
<LMM/ED>

1008   COFFIN, THOMAS E., and SAM TUCHMAN. "Rating Television
        Programs for Violence: A Comparison of Five Surveys." *Journal of
        Broadcasting* 17 (Winter 1973):3-20.

1009   COLDEVIN, GARY D. "Anik I and Isolation: Television in the
        Lives of Canadian Eskimos--the Far North." *Journal of
        Communication* 27, no. 4 (1977):145-53.
        Describes the impact of the expanded availability of television
as a result of the Anik I satellite transmission system on the Canadian
Eskimo. Adults have an increased knowledge of national and
international affairs. Indicates critical sociopsychological effects on
Eskimo children, while adults retain traditional social customs and
environment. <JMF/ED>

1010 ____. "Can Television Influence People?" *Television and Families*
8, no. 1 (1985):34-36.

Discusses simultaneous airing by three commercial networks
and influence on viewers' attitudes of the Great American Values Test,
a thirty-minute informational program designed to affect viewer's value
about environmental issues, racial equality, and sexual equality. The
program's effectiveness in influencing behavior was proven by a field
experiment. <MBR>

1011 COMSTOCK, GEORGE, and ROBIN E. COBBEY. "Television
and the Children of Ethnic Minorities." Paper presented at the 61st
annual meeting of the Association for Education in Journalism,
Seattle, Washington, 13-16 August 1978. [ERIC: ED168002]

A typical behavioral effect may be associated with the
relationship between ethnic minority children and television viewing.
Other differences may include a different orientation toward the
medium, different tastes and preferences, and different information
needs. Similarities between "majority" and "minority" children,
however, include a common pattern of parental concern, limited
parental control, and shared awareness of the potential for parental
influence over impact on attitudes and behavior. <AU/ED>

1012 COMSTOCK, GEORGE, and ELI A. RUBINSTEIN, eds.
Television and Social Behavior: Reports and papers. Vol. 1, *Media
Content and Control* Rockville, Md.: National Institute of Mental
Health, 1972.

A technical report to the Surgeon General's Scientific Advisory
Committee on Television and Social Behavior. This important and
widely debated document includes "Media Content and Control,"
"Television and Social Learning."

1013 COSGROVE, MICHAEL, and CURTIS MC INTYRE. "The
Influence of 'Mister Rogers' Neighborhood' on Nursery School
Childrens Prosocial Behavior." Paper presented at the Biennial
Southeastern Conference of the Society for Research in Child
Development, Chapel Hill, N.C., March 1974. [ERIC: ED097974].

Unpublished; available through ERIC. Results of this study
indicate that nursery school children viewing network programming *can*
benefit from viewing programs designed to teach prosocial behavior.
Younger children, however, do not obtain greater benefits than older
children from network programming. <CS/ED>

1014 COVER, JEANNE. "Theological Reflections: Social Effects of Television." *Religious Education* 78, no. 1 (1983):30-49.

Analysis of (1) ideologies of power and consumerism believed to govern and propagate through television and (2) the subservience of these ideologies, and of media technology, to large global corporations. Examples are provided of what the author believes to be false values supported by television. <UN/ED>

1015 CULTURAL INDICATORS RESEARCH TEAM. "The Gerbner Violence Profile." *Journal of Broadcasting* 21, (Summer 1977):280-86.

1016 DATES, J. "Race, Racial Attitudes and Adolescent Perceptions of Black Television Characters." *Journal of Broadcasting* 24 (Fall 1980):549-60.

1017 DIETERICH, DANIEL, and LAUREL LADEVICH. "The Medium and the Message: Effects of Television on Children: ERIC/RCS Report." *Language Arts* 54, no. 2 (1977):196-204.

Exploitation of documentary film subjects and their interpretation by children. Both the dangers of documentary film production and broadcasting by television and the responsibilities concomitant with those activities are explored. Effects upon children are considered. <AU/KS/ED>

1018 DONAHUE, THOMAS R. "Television's Impact on Emotionally Disturbed Children's Value System." *Child Study Journal* 8, no. 3 (1978):187-202.

A study of the influence of television's behavioral models on institutionalized, emotionally disturbed children ages six to eleven. Particular investigation of children's perceptions and judgements of right and wrong, appropriate and inappropriate behaviors, are discussed. <SE/ED>

1019 DRABMAN, RONALD S., and THOMAS HANRALTY. "Does TV Violence Breed Indifference?" *Journal of Communication* 25, (Fall 1975):86-89.

1020 EAPEN, K.E. "The Cultural Component of SITE." *Journal of Communication* 29, no. 4 (1979):106-13.

Highlights of results of surveys on the impact/effects of the Satellite Instructional Television Experiment (SITE) programs on two Indian villages. Discusses problems in conducting research at the

149

village level and the significance of rural realities and values in such communication experiments. <JMF/ED>

1021 ELEEY, MICHAEL F., GEORGE GERBNER, and NANCY TEDESCO. "Apples, Oranges, and the Kitchen Sink: An Analysis and Guide to the Comparison of 'Violence Ratings.'" *Journal of Broadcasting* 17 (Winter 1973):21-31.

1022 ____. "Validity Indeed." *Journal of Broadcasting* 17 (Winter 1973):34-35.

1023 FRIEDRICH, LYNETTE K., and ALETHA H. STEIN. "Aggressive and Prosocial Television Programs and the Natural Behavior of Preschool Children." *Monographs of the Society for Research in Child Development* 38, no. 4, serial no. 151 1973.
    Study in which ninety-three children in a nine-week nursery school session were shown one of three types of TV programs: aggressive cartoons, prosocial programs, and neutral films. Prosocial behavior increased after exposure to the prosocial program among subjects of lower socioeconomic status but not among those of higher status. Home viewing patterns did not predict baseline behavior. <UN/ED>

1024 GERBNER, GEORGE.
    See entries 188, 427, 1021, 1022.

1025 GERBNER, GEORGE, and LARRY GROSS. "Living with Television: The Violence Profile." *Journal of Communication* 26, no. 2 (1976):172-99.
    Analyzes the long-range social effects of television viewing and the need for new assessment methodologies. <UN/ED>

1026 GERBNER, GEORGE, LARRY GROSS, MICHAEL F. ELEEY, MARILYN JACKSON-BEECK, SUZANNE JEFFRIES-FOX, and NANCY SIGNORIELLI. "One More Time: An Analysis of the CBS Final Comments on the Violence Profile." *Journal of Broadcasting* 21, (Summer 1977).

1027 ____. "TV Violence Profile, No. 8: The Highlights." *Journal of Communication* 27 (Spring 1977):171-80.

1028 GIFFORD, C.A. "Impact of Television on South African Daily Newspapers." *Journalism Quarterly* 57 (Summer 1980):216-23.

1029 GORDON, MARGARET T. "A Countervalence in the Great Television Effects Debates." *Contemporary Sociology* 15, no. 2 (1986):182-84.

A review essay on Sandra J. Ball-Rokeach, Milton Rokeach, and Joel W. Grube, *The Great American Values Test: Influencing Behavior and Belief through Television* (New York: Free Press, 1984). The production of a thirty-minute television documentary on U.S. values is described, along with the methodology used to follow it up. The program, dealing with such contemporary issues as ecology, and equality, and designed to provoke self-confrontation, starred actor Ed Asner and news anchor Sandy Hill. Praised as an example of "extremely careful research," whose concern for ethics is exemplary. <UN/GD>

1030 GRADY, B.K. "What Is TV's Reality Doing to Students' Perception of the Real World?" *Etc.* 39 (Summer 1982):151-58.

1031 GRANZBERG, GARY, JACK STEINBRING, and JOHN HAMER. "New Magic for Old: TV in Cree Culture--the Far North." *Journal of Communication* 27, no. 4 (1977):145-57.

Impact/effects of television on Cree Indians within their own cultural context. Traditional Cree concepts about communication cause them to take television literally, to idolize superhero characters, to read special messages about behavior requirements into programming, and to be concerned about its potential harm to children. <JMF/ED>

1032 GREENBERG, B.S., and C.E. WOTRING. "Television Violence and Its Potential for Aggressive Driving Behavior." *Journal of Broadcasting* 18 (Fall 1974):473-80.

1033 HAWKINS, ROBERT P., and SUZANNE PINGREE. "Some Processes in the Cultivation Effect." *Communication Research* 7, no. 2 (1980):193-226.

Elaborates on cultivation hypothesis that heavy TV viewers incorporate biases present in television content into their own constructions of reality. Suggests that the integration of discrete television events into social reality beliefs requires cognitive skills not available to and unused by younger children. <JMF/ED>

1034 ____. "Uniform Messages and Habitual Viewing: Unnecessary Assumptions in Social Reality Effects." *Human Communication Research* 7, no. 4 (1981):291-301.

Challenges two assumptions of the Gerbner cultivation analysis: that commercial television is uniform in its symbolic messages about society's values, and that television viewing is habitual (ritual) rather than selective. Overall, both assumptions are challenged as flawed; discarding them, however, strengthens rather than weakens the cultivation hypothesis. <PD/ED>

1035 HOYT, J.L. "Courtroom Coverage: The Effects of Being Televised." *Journalism Quarterly* 58 (Winter 1981):582-88.

1036 HUR, K.K "Impact of 'Roots' on Black and White Teenagers." *Journal of Broadcasting* 22 (Summer 1978):289-98.

1037 HUR, K.K., and J.P. ROBINSON. "Uses and Gratifications Analysis of Viewing of 'Roots' in Britain." *Journalism Quarterly* 58 (Winter 1981):582-88.

1038 JACKSON-BEECK, M., and J. SOBEL. "Social World of Heavy Television Viewers." *Journal of Broadcasting* 24 (Winter 1980):5-11.

1039 KANG, JONG GEUN, and MICHAEL MORGAN. "Cultural Clash: U.S. Television Programs in Korea." Paper presented at the 69th annual meeting of the Association for Education in Journalism and Mass Communication, Norman, Oklahoma, 3-6 August 1986.

A study examined the influence of U.S. media on the values, morality, and traditions of other countries, and specifically the effects of American television on Korean values through the U.S. Forces Korean Network. Findings suggested that heavy viewers of U.S. programs are more likely to take liberal positions on various social issues than are light viewers and that U.S. programs are contributing to the Westernization of traditional cultures. <SRT/GD/ED>

1040 LECKENBY, J.D., and S.H. SURLIN. "Incidental Social Learning and Viewer Race: 'All in the Family' and 'Sanford and Son'. *Journal of Broadcasting* 20 (Fall 1976):481-94.

Study employed 781 racially and economically mixed respondents from Chicago and Atlanta. Findings suggest that high-frequency viewers of both programs find them entertaining and think they are realistic depictions of the groups portrayed. Researchers perceive frequent viewing to be influential in determining authoritarian attitudes and suggest further investigation of media effects. <KS/ED>

1041 LEE, E.B., and L.A. BROWNE. "Television Uses and Gratifications among Black Children, Teenagers and Adults." *Journal of Broadcasting* 25 (Spring 1981):203-8.

1042 LULL, JAMES. "The Social Uses of Television." *Human Communication Research* 6, no. 3 (1980):197-209.
    Supports a typology of the social uses of television using ethnographic research and gratifications literature. Demonstrates that audience members create specific and sometimes elaborate practical actions involving television to gratify particular needs in family viewing. <JMF/ED>

1043 MALIK, M.F. "Television Content." Quebec, Canada, 1978. [ERIC: ED213386].
    Focusing upon changes in the minds of the audience, this study of the impact of television programs provides a general analysis of the perceptual spectrum of the television audience and its values, preferences, and attachments to the content of television programming. Includes bibliography. <CHC/ED>

1044 MARK, M.M. Review of *The Great American Values Test - Influencing Behavior and Belief through Television,* by Sandra J. Ball Rokeach, Milton Rokeach, and Joel W. Grube. *Public Opinion Quarterly* 50, no. 2 (1986):280-82.

1045 MOSCHIS, GEORGE P., and ROY L. MOORE. "A Longitudinal Study of Television Advertising Effects." *Journal of Consumer Research* 9, no. 3 (1982):279-86.
    Study examined the short- and long-term effects of TV advertising in four areas: (1) consumer role perceptions, (2) normative consumer activities, (3) materialistic values, and (4) sex-role perceptions. TV advertising appeared to affect the development of materialism and traditional sex-roles when parents did not discuss consumption matters with their children, perhaps placing subjects at the mercy of advertising. <UN/ED>

1046 O'CONNELL, SHELDON. "Television and the Canadian Eskimo: The Human Perspective--the Far North." *Journal of Communication* 27, no. 4 (1977):140-44.

Describes a study of the impact of the first year of television on an Eskimo community by comparing the residents' responses with those of inhabitants of a community without television. Responses indicate a social impact on specific attitudes, but an overall retention of basic Eskimo values. <JMF/ED>

1047   PEI, MARIO.   "Blurred Vision: The Disturbing Impact of Electronic Media." *Change* 8 (November 1976):42-47.

The impact of radio and television on spoken and written language is exposed by a professor emeritus of romance philology. Degeneration of the language is linked with degeneration of customs and moral standards, and with the advent of electronic media. <LBH/ED>

1048   PIEPE, ANTHONY, JOYCE CROUCH, and MILES EMERSON. "Violence and Television." *New Society* 41(14 September 1977):536-38.

Replication of Gerbner and Gross's thesis of an association between heavy television viewing and identification with the victims of violence.   Testing of this idea in a British context failed to replicate Gerbner and Gross's findings, although strong associations were found between area of residence and a perception of the environment as violent or threatening.   Failure to replicate *may* be due to cultural differences in U.S. and British television.   Eight tables. <UN/ED>

1049   PINGREE, SUZANNE, and ROBERT HAWKINS.   "U.S. Programs on Australian Television: The Cultivation Effect." *Journal of Communication* 31, no. 1 (1981):97-105.

Study of effects of American television programs on Australian children.   Concludes that the cultivation of beliefs about the world, at least in cases of violence and crime, does occur even when the messages are imported from another country. <PD/ED>

1050   PRIDE, W.M.   "Possible Effects of Major Criminal Events on Audience Size and Channel Switching." *Journalism Quarterly* 54, (Winter 1977):773-76.

1051   REIN, D.M.   "Impact of Television Violence." *Journal of Popular Culture* 7 (Spring 1974):934-45.

1052   SILVERMAN, L.T., and J.N. SPRAFKIN.   "Effects of 'Sesame Street's' Prosocial Spots on Cooperative Play between Young Children." *Journal of Broadcasting* 24 (Spring 1980):135-57.

1053   STOLTE, DIETER.   "Learning to Live with Television."   *EBU Review* 25, no. 2 (1974):32-33. [ERIC: EJ098154].

A discussion of the effects of television upon West German society in the early 1970's. <HB/ED>

1054   SURLIN, STUART H.   "Selective Exposure to Discrepant Entertainment and News/Documentary Television Programs." Paper presented at the annual meeting of the Speech Communication Association, Washington, D.C. 1977.   [ERIC: ED149396].

Unpublished; available through ERIC.   Study tests the hypothesis that discrepant information will reach the desired audience when presented within a news/documentary program instead of through entertainment programming.   Low-authoritarian television viewers tended to prefer to receive discrepant information from a news/documentary program rather than from entertainment.   This same pattern held true, but to lesser degree, with high-authoritarian TV viewers.   One finding is that prior knowledge of program content affects one's desire to watch. <RL/ED>

1055   TAN, A.S.   Review of *The Great American Values Test-Influencing Behavior and Belief through Television*, by Sandra J. Ball Rokeach, Milton Rokeach, and Joel W. Grube. *Journal of Communication* 36, no. 1, (1986):149-51.

1056   TRACEY, MICHAEL.   "The Poisoned Chalice?:   International Television and the Idea of Dominance." *Daedalus* 114, no. 4 (Fall 1985):17-56.

The spread of North Atlantic culture across cultural boundaries is examined.   The television viewing habits of non-European/American nations generate a one-way flow of entertainment programs from the North Atlantic basin to the rest of the world. UNESCO figures are used to support this assumption.   Impact of Western-made videocassettes on traditional third world societies and values is also discussed. <UN/ED>

1057   WEISS, WALTER.   *Effects of the Mass Media on Communication.* New York: City University of New York/Hunter College, 1966.

Television, and indeed all mass media, may generate changes in cognition and comprehension, effect emotional arousal, stimulate sex behavior identification, and catalyze changes in allocation of time, consumer purchase, and voting behavior.   Document is a *survey* of literature on the effects of mass media, including some clarification of the television and aggression research during the 1960's. <MM/ED>

1058 WOTRING, C.E., and D.T. PORTER. "Effects of Televised Consequences of Aggression upon Physiological Arousal (Heart Rate)." *Communication Quarterly* 26, (Spring 1978):57-63.

1059 WURTZEL, ALAN. "Television Violence and Aggressive Behavior." *Etc.* 34 (June 1977):212-25.

II H. REGULATION, LAW, AND COURTROOM COVERAGE

1060 ANDERSON, JUDY. "Off-Air Videotaping: Are You Guilty of Copyright Violations?" *Public Relations Journal* 40, no. 9 (1984):26-27.

Use of off-air videotape without permission, although becoming common (as of this article's publication), is illegal. Obtaining permission to use broadcast materials is obtained step by step. The author argues that violations deprive other professionals of a portion of their livelihood and that such practice tarnishes the ethics and standards of the profession and of specific individuals. <AU/ED>

1061 BARBER, SUSANNA. *News Cameras in the Courtroom: A Free Press Fair Trial Debate.* Norwood, N.J.: Ablex, 1986.

Analysis of the free press-fair trial debate about the presence of news cameras in courtrooms. First comprehensive volume to discuss the issue from historical, legal, and social scientific perspectives. Sections include "Background to the Courtroom Cameras Debate." "Constitution Issues and Popular Arguments," "Summary of Research," "Focus Changes from Courtroom to the Audience," and a bibliography. <PR/ED>

1062 BEZANSON, RANDALL P., and GILBERT CRANBERG, and JOHN SOLOSKI. *Libel and the Press: Setting the Record Straight.* Minneapolis: Silha Center Publications, 1985.

A detailed analysis of all libel cases decided from 1974 to 1984, including results of surveys and interviews with plaintiffs, defendants, and attorneys. <SCP>

1063 BITTNER, JOHN R. *Broadcast Law and Regulation.* Englewood Cliffs, N.J.: Prentice-Hall, 1982.

1064 BURROWS, JOHN. *A Journalist's Guide to the Law.* New Zealand: N.Z. Training Board, 1982.

1065 CANNON, BRADLEY C. "The FCC's Disposition of 'Fairness Doctrine' Complaints." *Journal of Broadcasting* 13 (Summer 1969):315-24.

1066 CHAMBERLIN, BILL R., and CHARLENE J. BROWN, eds. *The First Amendment Reconsidered: New Perspectives on the Meaning of Freedom of Speech and Press.* New York: Longman, 1982.

1067 DENNIS, EVERETTE, DONALD GILLMOR, and DAVID GRAY, eds. "Had Black Ruled in Branzburg." In *Hugo Lafayette Black and the First Amendment: "No Law Means No Law."* Dubuque: Iowa State University Press, 1978.

1068 DEVOL, KENNETH S. *Mass Media and the Supreme Court.* Hastings-on-Hudson, N.Y.: Hastings House, 1978.

Updated to include major Supreme Court cases through 1986. Provides collection of major cases and selected reprints of important articles from leading law journals about obscenity, censorship, libel, right of privacy, and other First Amendment problems. Virtually all chapters mention television, but the final chapter "Trial by Television" is particularly relevant. <PR/ED>

1069 DILL, BARBARA. *The Journalist's Handbook on Libel and Privacy.* New York: Free Press, 1986.

1070 FELDMAN, CHARLES, and STANLEY TICKTON. "Obscene/Indecent Programming: Regulation of Ambiguity." *Journal of Broadcasting* 20 (Spring 1976):273-82.

1071 FELSENTHAL, NORMAN A. "Cherry-Picking, Cable, and the FCC." *Journal of Broadcasting* 19 (Winter 1975):43-53.

1072 FLOREN, LEOLA. *The Camera Comes to Court.* Columbia, Mo.: Freedom of Information Center, 1978. [ERIC: ED163559]
     After the Lindbergh kidnapping trial in 1935, the American Bar Association sought to eliminate electronic equipment from courtroom proceedings. A 1965 Supreme Court decision encouraged the banning of television cameras at trials as well. Some regulatory bodies have concluded that recording the proceedings of appellate courts is acceptable, but since the effect of electronic equipment on people in trial situations in unknown, those courtrooms must be kept clear of potential distractions. <TJ/ED>

1073 GARAY, RON. "The FCC and the U.S. Court of Appeals: Telecommunications Policy by Judicial Decree?" *Journal of Broadcasting* 23 (Summer 1979):301-18.

1074 GERALD, J. EDWARD. *News of Crime: Courts and Press in Conflict.* Westport, Conn.: Greenwood Press, 1983.
     Describes measures taken by the courts to maintain both the right to a fair trial and the right of the press to cover important public decisions, such as significant trials. Author contrasts rigid, formal structure of the bar to voluntary, laissez-faire system of journalism. <RR/ED>

1075 GILLMOR, DONALD M., and THEODORE L. GLASSER. *Mass Media Law, 1986.* Minneapolis: Silha Center Publications, 1986.
     A comprehensive listing of the best of both legal and mass communication literature on freedom of expression, the judicial process, and constitutional, administrative, and media law. <SCP>

1076 GIRARD, TOM. "Not in the Murrow Tradition: the '60 Minutes' Libel Case." *Variety,* 15 June 1983, 39.

1077 GLANCY, DOROTHY. "Invention of the Right to Privacy." *Arizona Law Review* 21, no. 1 (1979):1-39.

1078 GOLDMAN, KEVIN. "Network News Units under Legal Siege: Lawyers Go Hand-in-Hand." *Variety,* 19 January 1983, 1.

1079 _____. "Westmoreland's Attorney Asks Look at CBS 'Note.'" *Variety,* 18 May 1983, 45.

1080 GOLDMAN, NEAL M. "Tests of Media's 1st Amendment Rights Increasing." *Television-Radio Age,* 20 February 1984, 48.

1081 GORDON, DAVID. *Problems in Law of Mass Communication: Programmed Instruction.* Mineola, N.Y.: Foundation Press, 1982.

1082 HAGER, PHIL. "Advertising Cuts Lawyers' Fees, Study by FTC Finds." *Los Angeles Times,* 7 December 1984, sec. 1, 1.

1083 HALL, CLAYTON, W., Jr., and ROBERT BOMI D. BATLIVALA. "The Prime Time Rule: A Misadventure in Broadcast Regulation." *Journal of Broadcasting* 17 (Spring 1973):215-22.

1084 HOLSINGER, RALPH L. *Media Law.* New York: Random House, 1986.
       Introductory media law textbook that combines the casebook and narrative approaches. Aimed at undergraduate communication students but equally useful to broadcast professionals. <PR/ED>

1085 HOYT, JAMES L. "Courtroom Coverage: The Effects of Being Televised." *Journal of Broadcasting* 21 (Fall 1977):487-95.

1086 JACOBSON, ROBERT. *Municipal Control of Cable Communications.* New York: Praeger, 1977.
       Should cable systems be municipally owned? The author argues that cable television has not lived up to our high expectations for it. He concludes that cable's present profit orientation will never yield the level of service this technology is capable of providing. <CC/ED>

1087 JASSEM, HARVEY C. "An Examination of Self Regulation of Broadcasting." *Communications and the Law* 5, no. 2 (1983). [ERIC: ED235524]
       In 1928, the National Association of Broadcasters (NAB) developed a voluntary code of ethics to reduce public criticism of radio. Although the code appears to have had some positive impact on broadcast content, that impact was unenforceable and was designed to meet the interests of broadcasters. When the NAB disbanded its Code Authority Board in 1983, the loss of the NAB's codes did not, nor should not, significantly alter public protection. <HTH/ED>

1088   JOHNSON, NICHOLAS. "I Dissent." *Etc.* 32 (Spring 1975):273-75.

1089   JONES, ERIN. *Earth Satellite Telecommunications Systems and International Law.* Austin: University of Texas, 1970.

1090   KAPLAN, PETER. "The Westmoreland-CBS Case: TV Is the Center and Messenger of Trial." *New York Times,* 15 October 1984, sect. 2, p. 6.

1091   KENDALL, JOHN. "DeLorean Tapes--How Real Is the Plot?" *Los Angeles Times,* 31 October 1983, sec. 2, 1.

1092   KUPFERBERG, SETH. "Libel Fever." *Columbia Journalism Review* 20, no. 3 (September-October 1981):36-40.

1093   LAHAV, PNINA, ed. *Press Law in Modern Democracies.* White Plains, N.Y.: Annenberg-Longman Communication Books, 1985.

1094   LAWTON, SHERMAN P. "Who's Next? The Retreat of Canon 35." *Journal of Broadcasting* 42, no. 2 (1958):289-94.
       Survey of three hundred attorneys and thirty judges synthesizes attitudes about still photography, motion pictures, and live television in the courtroom. <RR/ED>

1095   LOFTUS, JACK. "NAB Fattens Rep. Rinoldo's Kitty during Debate on Broadcast Deregulation." *Variety,* 28 March 1984, 47.

1096   MADDOX, LYNDA M., and ERIC J. ZANOT. "Suspension of the NAB Code and Its Effect on Regulation of Advertising." *Journalism Quarterly* 61, no. 1 (1984):125-30, 156.
       Traces events leading to the suspension of the television code of the National Association of Broadcasters in 1982. Evaluates changes that have occurred in the resulting informal and formal regulation of advertising. <FL/ED>

1097   MESKE, MILAN. "Broadcasting and the Law of Defamation." *Journal of Broadcasting* 15 (Summer 1971):331-46.

1098   _____. "Editorial Advertising and the First Amendment." *Journal of Broadcasting* 17 (Fall 1973):417-26.

1099 MIDDLETON, KENT, and WILLIAM CHAMBERLAIN. *Law of Public Communication*. White Plains, N.Y.: Longman, 1987.

1100 MILLS, ROBERT W. "Radio, Television and the Right of Privacy." *Journal of Broadcasting* 13 (Summer 1960):51-61.

1101 MINNICK, WAYNE C. "The U.S. Supreme Court on Libel." *Quarterly Journal of Speech* 68 (November 1982):384-96.

1102 MINOW, NEWTON N. *Equal Time: The Private Broadcaster and the Public Interest*. New York: Atheneum, 1964.

1103 MUNDT, W.R., and E.J. BROUSSARD. "The Law/Ethics Dichotomy." *L.S.U. School of Journalism Research Bulletin* 2, no. 4 (1979).

Measuring disparity between journalistic attitudes toward law and ethics, the authors examined 241 journalism students' attitudes toward invasion of privacy by broadcast and print media. Eight cases representing the four torts that together form privacy law were used. In the estimation of respondents, conduct of the journalists in each case was seen as much more clearly legal than ethical. Overall suggestion is that journalists see the law as more forgiving than their professional colleagues. <UN/ED>

1104 MURAVCHIK, J., and J.E. HAYNES. "CBS vs. Defense." *Commentary* 72 (September 1981):44-55.

1105 NATIONAL ASSOCIATION OF BROADCASTERS. *The Challenge of Self-Regulation: NAB Radio and Television Codes in Review*. Washington, D.C.: National Association of Broadcasters, 1966.

A brief and *somewhat* dated pamphlet on the television and radio codes of the NAB.

1106 NELSON, HAROLD L., and DWIGHT L. TEETER, Jr. *Law of Mass Communications: Freedom and Control of Print and Broadcast Media*. New York: Mineola Foundation Press, 1982.

1107 OVERLAND, D. "Great Watergate Conspiracy! A TV Blitzkrieg?" *Contemporary Rhetoric* 233 (July 1978):29-32.

1108   PAUST, J.J. "International Law and Control of the Media: Terror Repression and the Alternatives." *Indiana Law Journal* 53 (Summer 1978):619-777.
       Special Issue: Terrorism and the Media.

1109   PEMBER, DON R. *Mass Media Law*. 4th ed. Dubuque, Iowa: Wm. C. Brown, 1987.
       Chapters on regulation of advertising, broadcasting, and media as a business; copyright; obscenity; free press and fair trial; protection of news sources and contempt of court; gathering information; records and meetings; invasion of privacy; libel; freedom of the press; and the American legal system. <ED>

1110   PERSKY, JOEL. "Self-Regulation of Broadcasting--Does it Exist?" *Journal of Communication* 27, no. 2 (1977):202-10.

1111   POLLAY, RICHARD W., JUDY ZAICHKOWSKY, and CHRISTINA FRYER. "Regulation Hasn't Changed TV Ads Much." *Journalism Quarterly* 57 (Autumn 1980):438-46.

1112   POWELL, JON T. "Protection of Children in Broadcast Advertising: The Regulatory Guidelines of Nine Nations." In *Advertising Law Anthology*. Washington: International Library, 1974.

1113   RIPLEY, JOSEPH M. "Policies and Practices Concerning Broadcasts of Controversial Issues." *Journal of Broadcasting* 9, no. 1 (1964-65):25-32.
       Results of two surveys of American broadcasting stations in 1957 and 1959. Most broadcasters were found to have policies ensuring their communities fair treatment of both sides of an issue. But in practice, too few stations provided an adequate amount of time for broadcasts featuring controversial issues. <RR/ED>

1114   ROSE, P. "Cameras in the Chamber in 1980?" *Contemporary Rhetoric* 236 (January 1980):12-14.

1115   SADOWSKI, ROBERT P. "Defamation and Disclosure: A Broadcast Precedent for State Shield Laws" *Journal of Broadcasting* 17 (Fall 1973):436-46.

1116 SALHOLZ, ELOISE, ALEXANDER STILLE, and MORRIS HOLLY. "Turning an Eye on the Lurid." *Newsweek*, 7 May 1984, 83.

Live television coverage of trials of alleged rapists and child molesters, particularly by the Cable News Network, is debated in this half-page article. <DLM/ED>

1117 SHOOK, FREDERICK, and DAN LATTIMORE. *The Broadcast News Process*. Englewood, Colo.: Morton Publishing Co., 1982.

Within part 4, which considers ethics and regulation, are chapters on "Legal Considerations" and "Ratings vs. Professionalism." At the end of each chapter are exercises for students. Appendices include journalism codes of ethics. <DLM/ED>

1118 SIMON, RAYMOND. "Legal Aspects of Public Relations Practice." *Public Relations: Concepts and Practices*. New York: John Wiley, 1984.

1119 SNOW, MARCELLUS S. *Marketplace for Telecommunications: Regulation and Deregulation in Industrialized Democracies*. New York: Longman, 1986.

1120 SPERRY, ROBERT. "A Selected Bibliography of Works on the FCC and OTP: 1970-1973." *Journal of Broadcasting* 19 (Fall 1975):55-113.

1121 STEVENS, JOHN D. *Shaping the First Amendment: The Development of Free Expression*. Beverly Hills, Calif.: Sage, 1983.

1122 TIME. "Full Court Press on CBS. *Time,* 9 May 1983, 63.

Legal examination of the significant 1983 trial, *CBS v. General Westmoreland*, in which the U.S. Army General John Westmoreland alleged that his reputation and person had been gravely misrepresented by CBS-TV's news department. <ED>

1123 TUCKER, D.E., and J. SAFFELLE. "Federal Communications Commission and the Regulation of Children's Television." *Journal of Broadcasting* 26 (Summer 1982):657-69.

1124 TUCKER, ELIZABETH. "FCC Weighs 'Character' Issue: Significant Shift in Rules on Fitness to Hold License." *Washington Post,* 22 May 1985, 3.

1125   VARIETY. "Vietnam Jury at Attention as Westmoreland Testified: Sez TV Hurt Troop Morale. Westmoreland Was 'Rattlesnaked' He Says of Wallace Interview." *Variety*, 21 November 1984, 37.

1126   WESOLOWSKI, JAMES WALTER.   "Obscene, Indecent, or Profane Broadcast Language as Construed by the Federal Courts." *Journal of Broadcasting* 13 (Summer 1969):203-19.

II I. PUBLIC AND EDUCATIONAL TELEVISION

1127   AUFDERHEIDE, P.   "Public Television's Prime-time Politics." *American Film* 8 (April 1983):53-57.

1128   BURGELMAN, JEAN-CLAUDE. "The Future of Public Service Broadcasting: A Case Study for a 'New' Communications Policy." *European Journal of Communication* 1, no. 2 (1986):173-202.

1129   FLETCHER, J.E. "Commercial versus Public Television Audiences: Public Activities and the Watergate Hearings." *Communication Quarterly* 25 (Fall 1977):13-16.

1130   FORE, W.F. "Public Television: Good News and Bad News." *Christianity and Crisis* 34 (10 June 1974):128-31.

1131   GOLDIE, G.W.   "Slow Assassination of Public Service Broadcasting." *Contemporary Rhetoric* 237 (September 1980):138-42.

1132   HUBERT, DICK. "Public Television Doesn't Deserve Its Halo." *Public Relations Journal* 39, no. 11 (1983):50-51.
        A system such as public television, supported in large measure by tax dollars, tax free, and tax-deductible donations contains much ethical ambiguity. For example, rules at the Public Broadcasting

166

Service allow a liquor company to underwrite programming production; the same company cannot advertise hard liquor on commercial TV. Moreover, companies are, despite legalities, sponsoring programs that deal with their product or cause. <UN/ED>

1133   KAUFMAN, PAUL. "Reflections on Values in Public Television and Their Relationship to Political and Organizational Life." Corporation for Public Broadcasting, 1972. [ERIC: ED066918]

Unpublished; available through ERIC. Public broadcasting and educational television are struggling to define themselves: it is insufficient to say that public interest consists of what is interesting; neither is it simply a matter of fair representation of various ideologies. To all of these must be added the need for philosophical and spiritual inquiry "to produce sights generative of insights." <MG/ED>

1134   KOPKIND, ANDREW. "MacNeil/Lehrer's Class Act." *Columbia Journalism Review* 18, no. 3 (September-October 1979):31-38.

1135   NATIONAL NEWS COUNCIL. *Independent Documentarians and Public Television*. Minneapolis: Silha Center Publications, 1980.

The report of a National News Council task force that explored the nature and legitimacy of gate keeping criteria used by PBS to judge documentaries made by independents. <SCP>

1136   PRISUTA, R.H. "Impact of Media Concentration and Economic Factors on Broadcast Public Interest Programming." *Journal of Broadcasting* 21 (Summer 1977):321-32.

1137   UNGER, ARTHUR. "Carter's 'Inside Story' Keeps a Watchful Eye on Media Ethics." *Christian Science Monitor*, 27 April 1984, 21-22.

Hodding Carter's Public Broadcasting Service program "Inside Story" is considered useful in teaching the nation about media ethics. Carter, however, is chided for hosting a program *within* the mass media which seeks to be a dispassionate critic of the news media, particularly as he was also employed by ABC-TV and *Wall Street Journal*. Can PBS claim exemption from media biases hiding behind the "educational" posture? <DLM/ED>

II J. DOCUMENTS: CODES, DECLARATIONS, LAWS, HISTORY

1138 ABC TELEVISION NETWORK. *ABC Broadcast Standards and Practices.* New York: American Broadcasting Company, 1980.

1139 AMERICAN ANTHROPOLOGICAL ASSOCIATION. *Professional Ethics.* Washington, D.C.: American Anthropological Association, 1973.

1140 AMERICAN ASSOCIATION OF SCHOOL ADMINISTRATORS. *Statements of Ethics for School Administrators.* Arlington, Va.: AASA, 1976.

1141 AMERICAN BAR ASSOCIATION. *Model Code of Professional Responsibility and Code of Judicial Conduct.* Chicago: American Bar Association, 1980.

1142 AMERICAN MEDICAL ASSOCIATION. *Principals of Medical Ethics: Opinions and Reports of the Judicial Council.* Washington, D.C.: American Medical Association, 1971, 10-12.

1143 AMERICAN PSYCHIATRIC ASSOCIATION. *The Principles of Medical Ethics.* Washington, D.C.: American Psychiatric Association, 1981.

1144   AMERICAN   PSYCHOLOGICAL   ASSOCIATION.   "Ethical
Principles of Psychologists." *American Psychologist* 36 (June
1981)633-38.

1145   AMERICAN SOCIOLOGICAL ASSOCIATION. *Code of Ethics.*
Washington, D.C.: American Sociological Association, 1969.

1146   ASSOCIATION   OF   CONSULTING   MANAGEMENT
ENGINEERS. *Professional Responsibilities of Management
Consultants: Ethics and Professional Conduct.* New York: ACME,
1973.

1147   BARNOUW, ERIC. *The Image Empire: A History of Broadcasting
in the United States since 1953.* Oxford: Oxford University Press,
1970.

1148   ____. *Tube of Plenty: The Evolution of American Television.*
Oxford: Oxford University Press, 1975.

1149   BARROSO, PORFIRIO ASENJO. *Codigos Deontologicos de los
Medios de Comunicacion: Prensa Radio, Television, cine, publicidad
y relaciones publicas.* Madrid, Spain: Ediciones Paulinas, 1984.
        In Spanish. Barroso is one of the best scholars and collectors
of international and national codes of media ethics. This adaptation of
his Ph.D. thesis comparing national codes includes many documents
otherwise difficult to obtain, although few are translated from Spanish.
<ED>

1150   ____. *Fundamentos Deontologicos de las Ciencias de la
Informacion: Prensa, radio, TV, cine, publicidad y relaciones
publicas.* Barcelona, Spain: Editorial Mitre, 1985.
        In Spanish.

1151   BRUUN, LARS, ed. *Professional Codes in Journalism.* Prague,
Czechoslovakia: International Organization of Journalists, 1979.
        Codes from Finland, Poland, and international organizations
are appended to several articles about the history, scope, and structure
of national and international media codes, particularly journalistic
documents that are easily compared cross-culturally and internationally.
<ED>

1152 COMMUNIST PARTY OF THE SOVIET UNION. *Rules of the Communist Party of the Soviet Union.* Moscow: Novesti Press Agency Publishing House, 1986.

Since the Communist party directly or indirectly controls all Soviet institutions, the party rulebook, available in English, dictates the spirit, and in some cases the letter, of broadcast Soviet expression.

1153 INTERNATIONAL ORGANIZATION OF JOURNALISTS. *International Principals of Professional Ethics in Journalism.* Prague, Czechoslovakia: International Organization of Journalists, 1986.

1154 INTERNATIONAL PRESS INSTITUTE. *Press Councils and Press Codes.* 4th ed. Zurich, Switzerland: International Press Institute, 1966.

1155 JASSEM, HARVEY C. "An Examination of Self-Regulation of Broadcasting." *Communications and the Law* 5, no. 2 (1983). [ERIC: ED235524]

1156 JONES, J. CLEMENT, ed. *Mass Media Codes of Ethics and Councils: A Comparative International Study on Professional Standards.* Paris: UNESCO, 1980.

The subtitle reveals the structure and method of the book. Jones has collected and analyzed professional codes from fifty countries, summarized the nature of the role of press councils, and appended representative draft codes and national codes. He discusses the general qualities of national codes and highlights their unique histories, structures, or emphases. <ED>

1157 KITTROSS, J. MICHAEL, and CHRISTOPHER STERLING. *Stay Tuned: A Concise History of American Broadcasting.* Belmont, Calif.: Wadsworth, 1978.

Among the best and most widely used histories of radio and television up to 1978. Complete with chronologies and chapters on each period. <ED>

1158 KRETSINGER, E.A. "Some New Techniques in Profile Analysis." *Journal of Broadcasting* 13 (Fall 1969):389-95.

1159 MAC BRIDE, SEAN. *Many Voices, One World.* Paris: UNESCO, 1980.

Thorough documentation of what has been called "the MacBride Report," as drafted by the MacBride Commission, in consideration of such international problems as the social responsibility of the press and the new world information order. <ED>

1160 MERRILL, JOHN C. "A Semantic Analysis of the SPJ/SDX Code of Ethics." *Mass Comm Review* 9, no. 1 (9181-82):12-15.
Close inspection of the code and its language. Criticizes the code as being vague, overgeneralized, high sounding, and almost meaningless. Character-by-character analysis of the entire document. <UN/ED>

1161 NATIONAL ASSOCIATION FOR PRACTICAL NURSE EDUCATION AND SERVICE. *Code of Ethics for the Licensed Practical/Vocational Nurse.* New York: NAPNES, 1985.

1162 NATIONAL ASSOCIATION OF BROADCASTERS. "The Challenge of Self-Regulation: NAB Radio and Television Codes in Review." Washington, D.C.: National Association of Broadcasters, 1966.

1163 NATIONAL EDUCATION ASSOCIATION OF THE UNITED STATES. *Opinions of the Committee on Professional Ethics.* Washington, D.C.: National Education Association, June 1969.

1164 NORDENSTRENG, KAARLE. *The Mass Media Declaration of UNESCO.* Norwood, N.J.: Ablex, 1984.
Contains numerous international documents and comparative analysis of many multinational and national texts. Useful tables and comparative charts give overview of primary issues and themes contained within international declarations and codes. <ED>

1165 ORLIK, PETER. *Broadcast Copyrighting.* Boston: Allyn & Bacon, 1982.

1166 PUBLIC RELATIONS SOCIETY OF AMERICA. *Code.* New York: Public Relations Society of America, 1974.

1167 RADIO-TELEVISION NEWS DIRECTORS ASSOCIATION. "Code of Broadcast News Ethics." *Journal of Broadcasting* 13, no. 4 (1984):386-88.
Report by the RTNDA Ethics Committee in 1984 recommends the 1969 statement of standards be simplified and more widely distributed. Single copies of the code are available at no cost,

and multiple copies are twenty-five cents each from the RTNDA, 1735 DeSales St., N.W., Washington, DC 20036. <DLM>

1168 SMEYAK, PAUL G. *Broadcast News Writing.* 1977. [ERIC: ED136277]

Unpublished; available through ERIC. Appendices include the Radio-Television News Directors Association code of broadcast news ethics, the radio code, the television code of the NAB, and a statement of principles of the bench, bar, and press of the state of Kansas. <KS/ED>

1169 SOCIETY OF PROFESSIONAL JOURNALISTS/SIGMA DELTA CHI. "Code of Ethics." In *1984-5 Journalism Ethics Report.* Fort Washington, Pa.: National Ethics Committee of Society of Professional Journalists/Sigma Delta Chi, 1985.

The code, drafted in 1926 and revised in 1973, represents a vast membership of broadcast and print journalists. <DLM/ED>

1170 SWAIN, BRUCE M. *Reporters' Ethics.* Ames: Iowa State University Press, 1978.

Includes American Society of Newspaper Editors statement of principles (1975), SPJ/SDX code of ethics (1973), and codes of seven major newspapers as appendices. Broadcasting ethics and law are discussed within the body of the text. <ED>

1171 UNESCO. *Mass Media Codes of Ethics and Councils.* Edited by J. Clement Jones. Paris: UNESCO, 1980.

See entry 1156.

AUTHOR INDEX

Compiled by Julie McAdoo

Note: References are to entry numbers, not pages.

SUBJECT INDEX

Compiled by Julie McAdoo

Note: References are to entry numbers, not pages. Cross-references preceded by a section number are to headings on the Table of Contents: those without section numbers are to other headings in the Subject Index.